THE DRAMATIC ART
OF DAVID STOREY

Recent Titles in
Contributions in Drama and Theatre Studies

THE DRAMATIC ART OF DAVID STOREY

The Journey of a Playwright

Herbert Liebman

Contributions in Drama and Theatre Studies, Number 71

GREENWOOD PRESS
Westport, Connecticut • London

Library of Congress Cataloging-in-Publication Data

Liebman, Herbert.
   The dramatic art of David Storey : the journey of a playwright /
Herbert Liebman.
      p.   cm.—(Contributions in drama and theatre studies, ISSN
   0163–3821 ; no. 71)
      Includes bibliographical references (p.   ) and index.
      ISBN 0–313–29865–3 (alk. paper)
      1. Storey, David, 1933–   —Criticism and interpretation.
   I. Title. II. Series.
   PR6069.T65Z73 1996
   822′.912—dc20   95–45210

British Library Cataloguing in Publication Data is available.

Library of Congress Catalog Card Number: 95–45210
ISBN: 0–313–29865–3
ISSN: 0163–3821

First published in 1996

Greenwood Press, 88 Post Road West, Westport, CT 06881
An imprint of Greenwood Publishing Group, Inc.

Printed in the United States of America

The paper used in this book complies with the
Permanent Paper Standard issued by the National
Information Standards Organization (Z39.48–1984).

10 9 8 7 6 5 4 3 2 1

For
Heather,
Judd and Jesse

CONTENTS

ACKNOWLEDGMENTS

I would like to express my appreciation to Dr. Una Chaudhuri of New York University for her assistance and encouragement. Her knowledge of contemporary theater and her keen insights into the plays discussed have always provided me with direction. I would also like to thank Dr. Roger Oliver and Dr. Joseph Byrnes, both of New York University as well, for reading and critiquing an early version of the manuscript. In addition, I would like to thank the College of Staten Island and the Research Foundation of The City University of New York (CUNY) for its support. Outside of academe, I would like to thank Tom Noonan, the actor, director, and filmmaker, for teaching me much about the truly important elements of drama. In addition, I would like to thank the playwright Ed Bullins, from whom I learned the rudiments of playwriting at the lively but now defunct Writers' Workshop of the New York Shakespeare Festival, and the playwright Israel Horovitz, with whom I worked closely at the New York Playwrights' Lab at the Actors Studio. I would also like to thank my wife, Heather Denwood-Liebman, for her encouragement and sense of humor. Finally, I would like to thank Nina Pearlstein, Jean Lynch, and Mark Kane, all editors at Greenwood Press, for their assistance and support.

1

THE YOUNG NOVELIST
BECOMES A PLAYWRIGHT

Angus Wilson described the benefits of a working relationship between a novelist who is interested in developing the craft of playwriting and a professional theater group like The English Stage Company at The Royal Court as follows:

> One hour spent in rehearsal teaches a writer more about playwriting than a month of working in isolation. . . . The Royal Court scheme for presenting new English plays should attract established novelists, for it will give them the opportunity to learn the new craft and attain the London production that must be their goal and their just reward. (qtd. in Browne 18)

This is what happened to the novelist David Storey, and although other novelists' plays were presented by the Court—novelists like Doris Lessing, Edna O'Brien, and Angus Wilson himself—none has achieved the reputation and importance in the theater that Storey has attained.[1] He learned the craft of playwriting while continuing to write novels, and has had thirteen of his plays produced since 1966, when *The Restoration of Arnold Middleton* appeared at the Traverse Theatre in Edinburgh.[2] Most recently, *Stages* was produced in 1992 at the Cottesloe Theatre (a part of the Royal National Theatre complex) in London. The sheer size of his artistic output is all the more impressive when one considers that Storey was a relatively young man of thirty-three at the time of his first dramatic production, as well as an accomplished author with three important novels published—the first two having won respected literary awards.[3] In addition, his first novel, *This Sporting Life* (1960), had already been turned into a successful film (1963) produced by Karel Reisz, directed by Lindsay Anderson, and starring Richard Harris—a film for which Storey himself wrote the screenplay. Storey was clearly the kind of talented novelist that The Royal Court sought for developing into a successful dramatist. Moreover, as he continued to write plays, he continued to write fiction,[4] publishing five more novels, among them *Saville* (1976), for which he won the prestigious Booker Prize for Fiction.[5]

Virtually all of Storey's plays, as well as his fiction, investigate three major thematic concerns: the world of madness, the world of work, and the world of the family.[6] It is the purpose of this study, therefore, to group Storey's plays into these three categories, and to examine within each the development of Storey's technique as a dramatist as well as his evolving understanding of the thematic material that he is exploring.

For example, the dramatist's view of the world of the insane has darkened considerably during his career. In *The Restoration of Arnold Middleton* (1967), Storey's first produced play, Arnold manages after an agonizing struggle with schizophrenia to return to a modicum of sanity. In his most recently produced work, *Stages* (1992),

Richard Fenchurch, a novelist and artist like Storey himself, succumbs to the madness that has pursued him his entire life—a "blackness" from which he can find no escape and that had previously, albeit temporarily, engulfed his father, a coal miner like Storey's own father. *Stages* ends with a portrayal of madness even more horrifying than Arnold Middleton's, for Fenchurch, close to the end of his career and his life, has no prospect of recovery. In *Stages* there is not even a hint, however slight, of a possible restoration to sanity.

Within each of these categories, I intend to examine the plays following a chronological sequence based on the date of each play's initial production rather than its reputed composition, since Storey himself is not always certain when a particular play was originally written.[7] In addition, Storey acknowledges the importance of the collaborative process provided by his association with the members of The Royal Court in shaping the final version of his script. In response to the suggestions of his theatrical collaborators, particularly his principal director Lindsay Anderson, Storey revised his script as it was readied for production. This suggests an ongoing mode of revision, and the dating of the final script is more accurately assigned to the work's production than to the date of its original composition.   Ronald Hayman, in an interview with the playwright, learned that Storey considered Anderson to have a "Tolstoyan" approach in the development of a play, while he, Storey, worked from "a molecular viewpoint, starting off from a detail and working up towards a complete picture"; and in the context of this collaboration, Storey expressed his admiration for Anderson's "editorial" manner in the development of his plays ("Conversations with David Storey" 47–48).

For example, Anderson encouraged Storey to eliminate the character of Mr. Reardon in the film version of *In*

Celebration (1969) because of the need for greater concentration. The cut worked so well that Mr. Reardon was again removed some five years later in the New York City production of the play (Hutchings, *Casebook* 14).

In many instances, moreover, a play can be placed within more than one category, so that an element of arbitrary discretion must enter into the classification process. Storey's first play, *The Restoration of Arnold Middleton*, is a family drama with a number of interesting similarities to his plays that investigate the matrix of domestic life, but the thrust of the play—its principal dramatic emphasis—is to probe the question of madness, a concern that follows Storey throughout his career.

First I will consider the dramas of madness: *The Restoration of Arnold Middleton* (1967), *Home* (1970), *Sisters* (1978), and *Stages* (1992). Laura Weaver in her essay, "Madness and the Family in David Storey's Plays," has documented that the playwright's insight into and understanding of madness is quite similar to the conception developed and popularized by the British psychiatrist, R. D. Laing (Hutchings, *Casebook* 124–25). Laing's analysis of madness is discussed at length in his *The Divided Self: An Existential Study in Sanity and Madness* in which the psychiatrist maintains that the modern family unit, as well as the larger society of which the family unit is a part, imposes crippling and alienating psychological burdens upon its members, thereby contributing to the development of madness (36–38, 94–105, 188–90).

Next I will deal with the dramas of work: *The Contractor* (1969), *The Changing Room* (1971), and *Life Class* (1974). In each of these plays, the work process itself is exposed in often minute detail, whether it is the step-by-step erection of a wedding canopy, the pregame preparations and warm-ups of professional rugby players, or the instruction of art students in the drawing of a nude

model. In addition, I will here be dealing with Storey's so-
called plotless plays and invisible events, terms used
frequently by William Hutchings in his commentary on
the playwright (*The Plays* 67–69), as well as examining the
dramatist's artistic aesthetic that is explicated at considerable length in *Life Class*. [8]

Then I will deal with the dramas of the family: *In
Celebration* (1969), *The Farm* (1973), *Mother's Day*
(1976), *Early Days* (1980), and *The March on Russia*
(1989). Like Ibsen, Storey probes deeply into the complex
texture of family relationships, "peeling [off] layer after
layer of defensive psychological armor"[9] that separates
parents from their children and siblings from each other.
Moreover, the new educational opportunities offered
bright working-class children[10] further divided the young
from the old as the former moved into professional and
affluent lifestyles. Thus, the very fabric of the family is
torn apart, as the educated young function in worlds that
remain closed to their own parents.

In my final chapter I will assess David Storey's contribution as a late twentieth-century British playwright.
Although he lacks the unrelenting menace of Harold
Pinter, the linguistic eloquence of Tom Stoppard, or the
narrative invention of Caryl Churchill—perhaps his most
significant theatrical contemporaries—he has created a
world and characters just as varied as theirs, and he has
done so with important insight into the complex struggle
of ordinary men and women to survive. He has, as one
critic observed, brought us into a closer and warmer relationship with the world of "apparently unremarkable
people" (Shrapnel 181–87). He is, after all, England's pre-
eminent working-class playwright, and he deserves
recognition for his singular achievement.

Storey's experiments with technique and structure reflect a wide spectrum of literary influence, ranging from

dramatists like Henrik Ibsen, Anton Chekhov, and Bertolt Brecht to Samuel Beckett, Harold Pinter and Joe Orton, and the effects of this influence upon Storey will be examined within the context of the playwright's development.

Early on, Storey experimented with specific strategies, like offstage characters and events directly interacting with onstage activities and infusing them with a particular energy and tension. He also became exceptionally skillful in the handling of theater space and in the setting up of structures or the movement of people upon that space, and these events—the erection and disassembly of marquee for a wedding or the locker room activities of professional rugby players before and after a match—evoked a powerful central image that lingered in the minds of theatergoers after the narrative experiences of the particular productions were long forgotten. In fact, so compelling and impressive is this visual image in performance, that Katharine Worth notes that the "poetic" effect of the tent's erection and disassembly on stage in *The Contractor* might very well be impossible to experience by solely encountering it in the printed text (28).

More importantly, Storey experimented widely with naturalistic modes of dramatic presentation, achieving, in a number of instances, a kind of *cinéma-vérité* or documentary realism for the stage, particularly in *The Contractor* and *The Changing Room*. These particular experiments, although occurring relatively early in Storey's career, represent, as we shall see, his most important dramatic achievements.

In all Storey's work, moreover, there is, on the part of the principal characters, despite persistent feelings of intense isolation, a struggle for survival in a chaotic and unjust world. Often educational activity, particularly for the bright working-class youngster, is the principal agent of alienation. The young are estranged in their new life

while their working-class background continues to assert
its influence, undermining their balance in the middle-
class environment to which they have been gaining admission. Despite their newly acquired professional status
and material benefits as adults, they find such a world,
like Andrew Shaw in *In Celebration*, empty and unfulfilling. To make matters worse, their education makes a return to their former working-class world impossible,
thereby creating a permanent and deep psychic detachment between the children and their parents. In the
Storey world, the class into which one is born can neither
be transcended nor denied—to reject one's working-class
roots is a form of treachery, to accept them anew is psychologically impossible. A permanent condition of disquiet
and distancing develops, a frequent existential dilemma
occurring in both Storey's plays and novels.

A particularly poignant and representative example is
developed in a brief scene in the novel *A Prodigal Child*.[11]
Bryan, the novel's young hero, is temporarily "adopted"
out of his working-class home where his father is a hard-
drinking farm laborer, so that he can enjoy the benefits of
a public school education while living in relative affluence in the home of the childless Corrigans.[12]   At a late
point in the novel, Bryan returns home to be with his
family after the death of Mrs. Spencer, the wife of his father's employer. However, having lived in the home of
wealthy benefactors while attending Peterson, a prestigious public school, Bryan is now uncomfortable in his
paternal working-class home and is particularly uneasy in
the presence of his older brother, who is training to be a
prizefighter and is very much a representative working-
class youth:

The room was cold; he [Bryan] wondered why, in the circumstances, he'd troubled to come back: far better, he realized, to have gone to Chevet [the Corrigans' home].
"I slept in your bed last night," his brother said.
"Why?"
"I thought I'd have a change. You can sleep in mine, if you want," he added.
Bryan got up from the chair; he picked up his case and went to the stairs: he heard his brother poke the fire and, a few moments later, as he sat on his unmade bed and wondered which one of the two he ought to sleep in, his brother came in and stood in the door.
In the corner of the room, on the cupboard top construction which marked the rising of the stairwell, was the first box of paints given him by Mrs. Corrigan: something in the faded texture of the lid reminded him of the slightness of her build, of her querulous eyes, and in this featureless room . . . the feeling that he didn't belong anywhere intensified. (261–62)

This is indeed a poignant moment for Bryan and is the central, disquieting realization of the novel. The awareness that his brother has slept in his bed certainly suggests a desire on the part of the elder sibling to reunite with his now privileged brother, but to Bryan it becomes a form of violation—of his crude brother's unwelcome intrusion into his bed and into his world of privilege. The fact that his brother sleeps in Bryan's bed and then invites Bryan to sleep in his own bed suggests an almost erotic desire on the part of Bryan's sibling to seduce his brother back into his biological fold. Nonetheless, the offer to bridge the division between the two is futile, at least as far as Bryan is concerned. This realization of the gulf between him and his family is further sharpened by the presence of "the first box of paints" given to him by Mrs. Corrigan. The small gift sits there in the plain and simple bedroom, a reminder of the affluence to which Bryan will return when his brief visit home is completed, and, more importantly, of the deep separation that now exists between him and his biological family. He has been uprooted into a permanent state of uneasiness: he will never feel comfortable within the prosperous world of the Corrigans nor will he ever be able to return to the working-class world of his childhood.

There are, as is to be expected, correspondences between Storey's plays and his fiction, and to the extent that his novels intersect with and enrich our understanding of his dramas they too will be examined. For example, in *Present Times,* a novel published in 1984, Storey's fictional hero, Frank Attercliffe, aged forty-seven and, like Storey, an ex-professional footballer, goes to see a regional performance of David Storey's *The Family*—the novel's title for Storey's actual drama *The Farm*—in the north of England and comments directly on the play, admiring its ambiguous ending, and even going so far as to suggest that the acting may have saved the London production, but the artistic quality of the play itself ensured its successful production in Yorkshire (80–90). Thus we see Storey's fictional hero commenting on his actual dramatic productions—we have, in effect, Storey the novelist providing a commentary on Storey the dramatist. Storey the novelist is assuring us that Storey the playwright is so skillful in constructing his dramas that not even a relatively unsophisticated dramatic production in the north of England could diminish the artistic merit of his work. Admittedly here the commentary is without any critical significance—it is simply praise, perhaps aimed at those critics who have, for one reason or another, attacked the ending of *The Farm.*

Quite amusingly, the occasion of visiting Storey plays in novels appears to be a family tradition. Storey's brother, Anthony Storey, almost five years his senior, an ex-professional soldier, a lecturer at Cambridge, and a novelist in his own right, has the entire family, including

brother David, visit a performance of *In Celebration* that
is entitled *The Family* in Anthony's novel (*Brothers
Keepers* 90–91).

At any rate, Attercliffe, in *The Present Times*, loses his
home to his wife, an ex-mental patient savoring a cruel
retribution toward her husband out of all proportion to
whatever harm, real or imagined, her marriage has in-
flicted upon her. To make matters considerably worse,
Attercliffe has been dismissed as a sports reporter, sued
unjustly over a rightful legacy, and, most painfully, estranged from his two eldest daughters, although he is, by
any standard, a caring and devoted father.

Despite these difficulties, Attercliffe becomes a playwright and begins work attending rehearsals of his first
play which turns out to be David Storey's *The Changing
Room* (225–27). For Frank Attercliffe writing becomes a
total commitment as well as a mode of rescue from the
chaos engulfing him at the present moment of crisis in
Great Britain, a world of disingenuous liberal values, of
social disintegration, of rampant crime and racism—a
world, in short, where he must wait out the social turmoil
in the desperate hope that some measure of cohesion and
sanity will be restored. In the meantime, however,
Attercliffe can only survive because he *is* a playwright.
He confronts the chaos of his life and sustains himself
through the discipline of his art. In Storey's fiction the act
of writing plays sustains his hero as it had previously sustained Storey himself at the beginning of his career as a
writer.

As a young art student and weekend professional
rugby player, Storey has documented his own complex
transition in an autobiographical essay, "Writers on
Themselves: Journey through a Tunnel." Originally presented as a talk on the BBC Home Service, this account details Storey's life as a young man, when every Friday for

almost two years he was required to travel from London, where he was a scholarship art student at the Slade School of Art, to West Riding in the north of England, where he was under contract as a professional football player for the city of Leeds.[13] The journey for Storey became a metaphor "across the darkness of" his mind, a rite of passage between the two worlds pulling sharply at his consciousness: the physical, "masculine" world of the footballer, and the intuitive, "feminine" world of the artist.

Storey saw the actual four-hour journey, while he was seated in a "tiny lighted cell" with complete darkness on the outside, as a route of "metaphorical reality," a voyage from intuitive, artistic London, where he enjoyed a level of personal and creative freedom hitherto denied him, to the dark puritan terrain of the north, the world of his childhood, where physical labor was expected and art was viewed as an "evil" ("Writers on Themselves" 160). The narrow and repressive values communicated to the young in this harsh environment cannot be underestimated in terms of their importance in shaping the writer's future work.[14] He describes the profound unhappiness of his father, a miner nearing sixty, returning home "shattered" from the pits to see his son, a young man every bit as physically capable as he, drawing pictures and writing poems.

Interestingly, this early confrontation between Storey and his father is of enormous significance as it reappears frequently in his work. In his most recent play, *Stages* (1992), Fenchurch, the hero, observes: "My father, back home from the coal-face at sixty-five to find me painting 'Osses! Clouds!—Bloody abstracts!'" (187). And in one of Storey's poems, "Piano," he yet again comments on this psychologically painful event: "Years later, / eroded by fatigue and fear, / he came home from work to find his son, / muscled for / the tasks that drove him to his knees, /

painting by the fire: a picture of clouds" (*Storey's Lives* 62).

Nevertheless, the two years of travel between London and Leeds were "the unhappiest" in his life as he attempted to reconcile the self-absorbed, intuitive dimension of his being with his hard, extroverted surface—and his surface had to be very hard indeed, for the game he played, professional rugby, is considered by many, including David Storey, to be the most violent of all professional sports. [15]

Storey tried to heal the rift by painting, but this only intensified his isolation, so he turned to composing a diary and then to his first novel, *This Sporting Life* ("Writers on Themselves" 160–61). Writing fiction, a more social activity to Storey than painting, rescued him from his isolation and despair ("Writers on Themselves" 161).

Storey's subsequent movement from fiction to drama is quite possibly a further effort on the writer's part to involve himself in a wider, more sympathetic world, thereby diminishing the alienation he experienced as a painter and football player. Fiction clearly is done alone, between the writer and the empty page; playwriting, on the other hand, involves a considerable number of individuals in the development of a text—directors, actors, designers, producers, and the live audience itself. Storey, the novelist-turned-playwright, may well have appreciated the widening world of his creative efforts.

Storey, on these weekend jaunts between London and Leeds, invariably brought with him a copy of Wyndham Lewis's *Rude Assignment: An Intellectual Autobiography*, published in 1950, which he claims to have read "six times" ("Writers on Themselves" 159). Strictly speaking, Lewis's book is less an autobiography than a celebration of intellectual vigor, particularly Lewis's own, in the "high brow" tradition of Western man, a tradition defined by

"Darwin, Voltaire, Newton, Raphael . . ." (Lewis 207). Lewis had previously contrasted the "high brow" to the mediocrity of "the low brow" bourgeoisie whom he despised as intellectually vacuous (Lewis 15). Considering Storey's background, it is rather curious that he identified so strongly with a patrician like Lewis, and one does justifiably wonder what the younger writer saw in the older man. Was it a form of defensive admiration fueled out of awareness of his working-class background? Indeed, if we are to understand Lewis fully, he would have considered Storey and the people in the mining towns of Yorkshire from which the playwright emerged as "no brows." Lewis writes:

> This classification [low brow] does not extend beyond the bourgeoisie. The working class of course does not count. The typical "low brow" would not like to think he shared his brow with *them*. They might, if it came to the point, be described as the "no brows." (15)

The many working-class characters in Storey's novels and plays—characters like the occasionally violent and often insensitive Arthur Machen and the dour Mrs. Hammond in *This Sporting Life* or the hard-working miner Mr. Shaw and his excessively hygienic wife in *In Celebration*—would find little sympathy with a writer as intellectually condescending and as culturally biased as Wyndham Lewis. Even Storey's educated heroes, individuals of considerable intellectual and artistic ability, like the Shaws' son Andrew, a solicitor-turned-artist, or Colin Pasmore, a university lecturer in history, who appears initially in the novel *Pasmore* and later reemerges in Storey's drama *The March on Russia,* would most likely be dismissed as "lowbrows," unworthy of serious examination and sympathy on Lewis's part.

Perhaps the element that so strongly appealed to Storey was neither the aesthetic that Lewis preached nor the depiction of intellectual rigor he so strongly cherished, but Lewis's conception of artists as isolated within society and in need of protection against the "alien" elements that surrounded them.

Lewis spent a number of summers in Brittany in Finisterre, which he defined as a "primitive society" (124), and he described an isolation experience similar in intensity to Storey's weekend bouts of alienation among his rugby teammates. The fishermen of Brittany, like the colliers in the north of England, brawled and drank, and "a stabbing was not an infrequent occurrence" (124). Ultimately Lewis claimed that "to spend so much time in contact with the crudest life is . . . wasteful of life" (126). These bitter thoughts do mirror to some extent Storey's own negative and unhappy feelings toward those with whom he played professional rugby on weekends. The footballers deliberately mistreated Storey because he was an art student, an activity they held in the deepest contempt. Furthermore, Lewis, like Storey, had been an art student at Slade, and this simple fact must have reinforced the otherwise peculiar identification that the working-class writer David Storey felt for the profoundly condescending Wyndham Lewis. Quite possibly, had the two met, Lewis would have dismissed Storey abruptly, since it is difficult to select two writers whose sensibilities and backgrounds are further apart than these two. Actually, in this specific regard, Storey is quite explicit on the connection to the older writer:

Wyndham Lewis's view of the artist as a man isolated in an alien society and therefore of necessity clothed in armour of the most rigid and impenetrable design, was an attitude to which I was invariably drawn. ("Writers on Themselves" 160)

As expected, a number of critics have compared the relative merits of Storey's fiction to his dramas. For example, on the basis of very thin evidence and a dismissive attitude toward the dramas, Mike Bygrave concludes that Storey is clearly superior as a novelist, but he does so grudgingly, for the fiction thus far published is, Mike Bygrave contends, more indicative of potential than of accomplishment (31–36).

Even Storey himself enters into the controversy, but sends out confusing signals. In his conversation with the critic Ronald Hayman, he observes that he prefers fiction: "I feel I am more a novelist than a playwright. The sentimental attachment is always to the novel" ("Conversations with David Storey" 47).[16] This clear declaration is somewhat modified by Storey's subsequent observation that drama and film have "more potential" than fiction, and his belief that the novel in England has no "future" (Gibb 9). Storey, being so talented in both fields, quite possibly feels superior as a novelist one day, as a playwright the next, the preference depending perhaps on the particular creative moment—what he is presently writing and how well the project is moving along.

A much more interesting approach is to see the two genres as complementary rather than as competing, and to view "all of his writings" as "of a piece," a critical position argued by Phyllis Randall (253). She sees strong similarities in characters, backgrounds, and incidents in both the fiction and the drama, and observes that the work in its entirety falls into two groupings: "the disintegration of the family" and "the disintegration of the individual personality, often to madness" (254). Janelle Reinelt sees continuity in many of the novels and plays and through "an intertextual reading" claims Storey has constructed a "master narrative" that "explores the failure of human subjectivity to conceive and design solid, secure structures of meaning" (Hutchings, *Casebook* 53, 69).

However, there are clear literary differences and concerns, particularly in matters of style and tone, between Storey the novelist and Storey the playwright. James Gindin has observed that Storey as a novelist "is more ruminative ... the structural ideas more explicitly developed," while his "drama has been most effective when it is furthest from his fiction, when the drama is most stark ... emphasizing the delineation of the situation or the phenomenon itself" (510–11).

To date, there has been surprisingly little scholarly response to a playwright of David Storey's importance. Aside from a relatively small number of significant articles,[17] only one text in the 1970s, a pamphlet, devoted itself exclusively to Storey's literary contribution, and this work is much more appreciative of his fiction, citing him as England's "first truly modern novelist," than of his plays, which are dealt with rather superficially.[18] The most important recent scholarly work has been the contribution of William Hutchings who has written the first full-length work devoted to Storey's plays and has subsequently edited a collection of critical writings on the playwright.[19]

Hutchings has treated Storey in an exhaustive manner, but his approach to the dramas is to some extent limited by a central concern of his analysis: he sees the offstage event—for example, the actual football game in *The Changing Room*—as an invisible occurrence that is central to the meaning the play. In response to this event, as well as to similar "invisible" events in other Storey plays, Hutchings argues that Storey constructs secular myths to enable his characters to find meaning in an essentially "desacralized" world (*The Plays of David Storey* 18–25).

While not denying the intellectual and cultural significance of Hutchings's analysis and the often important insights he provides, my approach is to see the event as part of Storey's complex dramaturgy and to compare it with similar invisible or offstage activities in the works of other important contemporary playwrights.[20] Storey is foremost a dramatist who seeks to discover within the structure of his play a form that corresponds to the particular theme that he is developing. Quite simply, the events that occur, both on- and offstage, are inextricably linked to the thematic focus evolving in the play. This is not to deny the myth-making elements in Storey's plays, or the absence of meaning in traditional ritual in the contemporary world—two observations that are central to Hutchings' thesis—but to clearly de-emphasize them in the study of the plays and their structures.

Obviously Storey is mixing and balancing onstage and offstage activity and allowing the energy communicating between the two perspectives to focus the movement in his dramas. The critic Hanna Scolnicov, in her discussion of space in the theater, provides specific language that is particularly helpful in dealing with a playwright like Storey, particularly in his manipulation of onstage and offstage activity. She emphasizes the balance struck between the action occurring on the stage, "the theatrical space within," and the action occurring off the stage, "the theatrical space without," and argues that each of these worlds is equally important and equally real (14–15).

For example, as the workers meticulously construct the tent in *The Contractor*, the events occurring during the marriage—a ceremony that is never seen—flow in upon the action occurring on stage and extend and enrich the drama's complexity. Similarly, in *The Changing Room*, the actual game, which is never seen, provides an offstage tension and reality against which the locker room activities of the footballers and their coaches are given shape and meaning. What occurs offstage is not "an invisible event" (*Casebook* 106) as Hutchings argues, but an organic element of the play's structure.[21]

Space in the theater is seen, therefore, as Scolnicov argues, as a "theatrical object in its own right" (25). What we see with our eyes and what we "see" in our imagination often flow into each other, the two perceptions mixing and contributing to a "synchronic" understanding of the play's complexity (25). Indeed, as we shall see, in a number of Storey's most important plays, works like *The Contractor* (1969), *Home* (1970), and *The Changing Room* (1972), the dramatist's use of space represents one of his most inventive and perhaps enduring dramatic achievements.

In the following chapters, Storey's three principal dramatic worlds—madness, work, and the family—will be examined in the context of the literary influences that have shaped the particular dramas as well as the playwright's developing thematic complexity. Finally, there will be a concluding discussion that will assess Storey's achievement as a playwright with a unified body of work. Of necessity, this assessment will be tentative, since Storey is still active as a dramatist, having produced *The March on Russia* in 1989 and *Stages* in 1992.

NOTES

1. Indeed, Angus Wilson's play, *The Mulberry Bush* (1956), directed by George Devine, was the first production of the newly formed English Stage Company at The Royal Court Theatre. Doris Lessing's *Each His Own Wilderness* and Edna O'Brien's *A Pagan Place* were produced in 1958 and 1972 respectively (Browne 103, 104, 111).

2. For the record, Storey has written fifteen plays, one of which, *The Phoenix*, was published only in an acting edition (Dramatic Publishing Company) in 1993 and has never been produced profession-

ally, although it has twice been presented by amateur groups, the Questors in Ealing in 1984 and Century Theatre on tour in Yorkshire in 1985 (*Phoenix* iv).   In addition, "Caring," an experimental one-act play, has been published (*Storey Plays: One*), but has never been produced.

3. *This Sporting Life* published in 1960 won the MacMillan Fiction Award; *Flight into Camden* also published in 1960 won the John Llewelyn Rhys Memorial Prize in 1961 and the Somerset Maugham Award in 1963; *Radcliffe*, his third novel, was published in 1963.

4. Storey's awards as a playwright are even more impressive: *The Restoration of Arnold Middleton* won the Evening Standard Award for the Most Promising Playwright (1967); *The Contractor* won the London Theatre Critics Award for Best Play (1970), and Writer of the Year Award from the Variety Club of Great Britain (1971); *Home* won The Drama Award from the *Evening Standard* (1970), and the Award from the New York Drama Critics Circle (1971); and finally *The Changing Room* in 1973 won the New York Drama Critics Circle Award (Hutchings, *Casebook* xviii–xix) .

5. Storey has also published a recent volume of poetry, *Storey's Lives: Poems 1951–1991* (1992).

6. Thus far, only three of Storey's fifteen plays do not fall within the thematic range defined in this study: *Cromwell* (1973) a Brechtian historical play written in free verse; *Phoenix* (1984), a conventional two-act play that attacks the philistine sensibilities of those who fund and thereby control subsidized theater in the north of England; and "Caring" (1992), a one-act, unproduced dramatic dialogue with Beckettian influences in its absence of action, the mysterious identity of the two speakers, and their frequent lapses of memory.

7. William Hutchings, in fact, provides a chronology of Storey's dramatic work, and in a number of instances the playwright himself cannot date certain works definitively (*The Plays* 10–11). But there is a more compelling reason to date the plays on the basis of production. Storey worked in a writers' theater, The Royal Court, and as a working playwright producing new dramatic material, he wrote and rewrote right up to the moment of production—even if the original script had been completed in a first draft some years in the past.

8. Hutchings identifies *Life Class* as "one of the most original and unusual works of metatheater in contemporary drama" (*Casebook* 108).

9. See, for example, Michael Billington, who identifies Ibsen's technique as of primary influence ("A Play Worth Having" 16A).

10. See Kerensky (xx) for a discussion of the Educational Act of 1944, which provided intellectually gifted working-class youngsters, like David Storey himself, with superior educational opportunities.

11. This autobiographical novel, published in 1982, is considerably less successful than *Saville*, initially appearing almost as an uninspired rewrite of the former book. The father in *A Prodigal Child*, however, is depicted as a poor farm laborer rather than, as in *Saville*, a miner. Nevertheless, in the Storey canon, *A Prodigal Child* is the most powerful and sustained example of the hero's erotic attachment to the older woman, a situation that is common in Storey's dramas and fiction, commencing with his very first published work, *This Sporting Life* (1960) and appearing with major thematic importance in his most recent production, *Stages* (1992).

12. Even on the very first day of Bryan's departure from his house to live with the Corrigans, he performs, in the company of Mrs. Corrigan, his benefactress and erotic obsession, an odious and unforgivable act by denying his own mother in the town's marketplace. Her presence clearly distresses him. "If anything, that glimpse of the shabbily-coated figure with its familiar stoop and the anxious, birdlike cocking of its head, reassured him that, even if there had been something to unite them in the past, there was nothing now" (185). Bryan has rather rapidly become a contemptible and ungrateful prig, although at the end of the novel he does make some attempt to reconnect with his roots.

13. According to his coach, Ken Dalby, David Storey was a fine athlete with exceptional promise. See Martha Duffy's "An Ethic of Work and Play." This essay is most informative on the playwright's personal attitudes toward sport and violence, subjects which appear with important thematic significance in both his dramas and his fiction.

14. John Stinson has noted that in the north of England the tight web of puritanical values exercised a persistent and pervasive influence upon the dramatist's characters. Even the young and gifted, like Storey himself, who are clever enough to pass the eleven-plus and earn the right to superior educational opportunities, cannot fully disconnect from the dreary and limited world of their working-class parents. This occurs because they discover that their new lives as professionals are

unrewarding. They have brought with them a considerable potion of "paternal venom" against artistic and intellectual work. This is, of course, paradoxical, since their parents wish them to succeed (131–143). Stinson quotes Storey's disturbing and perplexing observation about his own father: "A professional man, that's what he [Storey's father] wanted me to be, perhaps a teacher. And so I went to school. But I was confused as to what he did want. There was this chap down the street who was becoming middle class, had an office job, a bowler, and a little motor, the symbol of the middle class. And yet every time my father saw that man get in his car and drive past, he would emit the most violent sounds of rage and derision" (135). Those who wish to explore the consequences of the eleven-plus, and the alienating effect of education upon academically gifted working-class children, should read Storey's *Bildungsroman, Saville* (1976).

   15. Martha Duffy notes "Rugby League remains a private, insular British phenomenon, a deeply rooted part of working-class life north of the Trent, capable of arousing savage loyalties. Yet unlike soccer ... it has never been plagued by riots. Many, including playwright Storey, believe the game itself is so violent that the crowd is sated by it" (66). Furthermore, professional rugby should be distinguished from rugby union, a sportsmanlike, middle-class, and comparatively gentle game (69).

   16. The predilection for fiction is also indirectly supported in *Stages* (1992), an autobiographical play, where Fenchurch, the protagonist, identifies himself as a novelist and a painter but never as a dramatist.

   17. Of particular interest are the following works: Richard Cave, *New British Drama in Performance on the London Stage: 1970 to 1985* (New York: St. Martin's, 1988); Ruby Cohn, *Retreats from Realism in Recent English Drama* (New York: Cambridge UP, 1991); Ronald Hayman, *British Theatre since 1955: A Reassessment* (London: Oxford UP, 1979); Austin E. Quigley, "The Emblematic Structure and Setting of David Storey's Plays," *Modern Drama* 22 (1979): 259–76; Carol Rosen, *Plays of Impasse: Contemporary Drama Set in Confining Institutions* (New Jersey: Princeton, UP, 1983); and John J. Stinson, "Dualism and Paradox in the 'Puritan' Plays of David Storey," *Modern Drama* 20 (1977): 131–43.

   18. John Russell Taylor, *David Storey: Writers and Their Work, No. 239* (Edinburgh: Longman, 1974). Interestingly, the same writer's

earlier work, *The Second Wave: British Drama of the Sixties* (London: Methuen, 1971), dealt in a more interesting manner with the "elusive" dimension of Storey's plays (145).

19. William Hutchings, *The Plays of David Storey: A Thematic Study* (Carbondale: Southern Illinois UP, 1988); William Hutchings, ed., *David Storey: A Casebook* (New York: Garland, 1992).

20. Numerous playwrights have developed dramatic strategies similar to Storey's—strategies that create tension between those on stage communicating with or affected by those whose presence, although not seen, generates the energy that informs the movement of the drama. Among the many plays that can be cited are Beckett's *Waiting for Godot* (1954), Pinter's "The Dumb Waiter" (1957), Mamet's *American Buffalo* (1975), and Shepard's *Fool for Love* (1983).

21. As opposed to "theatre space," which Scolnicov calls "perceived space"—that which we can actually see—"the theatrical space" and "the theatrical space without" are "conceived space"—that which is extrapolated from the events on stage (14).

2

PLAYS OF MADNESS

In Storey's plays, as well as in his novels, madness is usually a significant concern. Indeed, in one early study of the playwright, a critic has observed: "In six of the first seven plays which Storey has written . . . at least one character is on the verge of insanity, an idiot or a certifiable lunatic. To grasp Storey's dramatic use of madness . . . is to understand an artist's attempt to reconcile himself to a bewildering universe where the line between sanity and insanity is often invisible" (Kalson 111). These comments, published in 1976, can be applied with equal accuracy to Storey's subsequent work.

For example, in Storey's novel, *Present Times* (1984), Frank Attercliffe, the novel's central character, has a wife who has been hospitalized as a result of a severe nervous breakdown, while Attercliffe himself struggles under intense stress to retain his own sanity in the midst of an array of frenetic and bizarre incidents in his personal and professional life. Indeed, the tension of the narrative in the novel is sustained to a considerable extent by the ever-present possibility that Attercliffe, despite his levelheadedness and maturity, will himself crack in response to the increasingly severe demands of his situation.[1]

However, for the purposes of this chapter, I have selected four plays where madness is present and focal, where the principal character or characters have indeed gone insane: *The Restoration of Arnold Middleton* (1967), *Home* (1970), *Sisters* (1980), and *Stages* (1992). In these four plays, further, Storey deals with madness from different perspectives. In his very first play, *The Restoration of Arnold Middleton*, he describes the descent into madness. For Arnold, as we first meet him, is, however troubled, still sane—a witty, bumbling, schoolmaster who collects numerous objects, like a suit of armor and a Lee-Enfield rifle that he deposits in a helter-skelter manner around his house, against the strong objections of his wife.   But Arnold is a man who is deeply distressed and uses his eccentricities to erect a barrier of protection around his troubled self.   The drama then traces his decline until he has withdrawn completely from those around him—his wife, his mother-in-law, his colleagues, and his students.   In this respect, the title, *The Restoration of Arnold Middleton*, is misleading, for there is certainly no "restoration" at the end of this drama.[2]

In *Home* we enter a world that appears normal, a world where two respectable English gentlemen sit in a garden in the sunlight to pass the time in idle chatter. They are, however, two madmen in a world of the mad, residents in a mental institution. This reality grows upon us slowly, as it grew slowly upon David Storey while he was writing his play, and its final realization contains considerable dramatic impact. The playwright tells us that he was halfway through the drama when he discovered that it "was taking place in a lunatic asylum" (Findlater 113). If what appears thoroughly normal is indeed utterly mad, then what is utterly mad can and does appear thoroughly

normal. This paradox, as we shall see, is inherently dramatic, for we are often in situations where we discover
that where we think we are—a park bathed in morning
sunlight—is quite different from where we actually are—
the grounds of a mental institution.

As *Home* examines a society, so *Sisters* examines a
single individual, Adrienne, whom we initially assume to
be the sole normal and dignified presence in an utterly
mad world. Adrienne, in need of refuge, has arrived
unwittingly at a suburban brothel, a so-called knock shop,
run by her sister Carol and her rough, ex-footballer
husband, Tom. The brothel is patronized by a wide range
of colorful characters. Among them are a sensitive and
young schoolmaster with a love for history and geology
(91), a cynical and obviously corrupt police officer, who
believes his participation in the "knocking shop" actually
sustains his "happy and . . . satisfactory marriage" (112),
and a married woman, Joanna, who identifies herself as
"an intermittent paying guest" (83) willing to participate
as a prostitute because her husband dislikes her (130).
Furthermore, the permanent residents of the brothel are
cared for by Mrs. Donaldson, who at first appears
grandmotherly, warm, and reassuring, an archetypal,
matronly presence. She also claims to be the mother of
Carol, Adrienne's sister (60), an announcement that
initially startles both us and Adrienne, who, we assume,
should at least be able to recognize her own mother, as
indeed her mother, Mrs. Donaldson, should be as equally
capable of recognizing her own daughter.[3] But the
brothel, like the lunatic asylum in *Home* is not
immediately identified for what it is, nor, for that matter,
are the characters immediately recognized for whom they
actually are. We must proceed further into the drama
before we realize where we are located and who the

individuals on stage are, the process of realization occurring, as in *Home*, slowly and incrementally.

Stages (1992), Storey's most recent dramatic exploration of madness, is a long, complex, one-act play that probes in detail the incestuous relationship between the principal character, Richard Fenchurch, and his mother-in-law, Isabella Corrigan,[4] whose death triggered Fenchurch's madness (205).[5] Yet madness for Richard is here a mode of survival ultimately expressed in the play's conclusion through the metaphor of "dancing" (219). All Richard can do at the end is dance to the painful memories of his life.

Before we begin discussing the four plays, however, it would be helpful to examine in somewhat more detail R. D. Laing's understanding of madness, since Storey has acknowledged that his own understanding of the experience of madness—an experience that he has dramatized frequently in his plays—is quite similar to Laing's conception.[6]

Laing's basic understanding of both the genesis and experience of madness is clarified succinctly in a series of prose poems or "patterns," as Laing more appropriately defines them, in his book *Knots*. A particularly representative example is the following:

There must be something the matter with him

    because he would not be acting as he does

       unless there was

      therefore he is acting as he is

      because there is something the matter with him

He does not think there is anything the matter with him

because

    one of the things that is

      the matter with him

      is that he does not think that there is anything the matter

        with him

therefore

      we have to help him realize that,

        the fact that he does not think there is anything

        the matter with him

        is one of the things that is

        the matter with him . . . (5).

This pattern crystallizes R. D. Laing's fundamental conception of madness. It is basically behavior that is unacceptable in terms of the norms of society, even though the individual performing that behavior "does not think" that he is mad. This is explicitly stated in the observation that society believes the individual "is acting as he is / because there is something the matter with him"; the fact that the individual performing the behavior deemed unacceptable does not "think there is anything" pathological in such behavior is further evidence of his madness. Ironically, and quite tragically, in Laing's view, the individual's acceptance of his conduct is used as evidence of his madness. Moreover, his behavior may be quite harmless to himself and to others, but it is still unacceptable, and society will, if necessary, "help him" to realize and appreciate his madness: society must teach the individual that the fact that he "does not think there is anything / the matter" is itself evidence that something is the matter. There is something sinister here, for behavior that is unacceptable is, in Laing's view, a *"political event "* [Laing's emphasis] and not a medical condition.   In fact, Laing argues, the condition "schizophrenia" does not exist:

> There is no such "condition" as "schizophrenia," but the label is a social fact and the social fact a *political event.*   This political event, occurring in the civic order of society, imposes definitions and consequences on the labeled person. It is a social prescription that rationalizes a set of social actions whereby the labeled person is annexed by others, who are legally sanctioned . . . to become responsible for that person. The person labeled is inaugurated not only into a role, but into a career of patient, by the concerted action . . . of family, G.P., mental health officer, psychiatrists . . . and often fellow patients.   The "committed" person labeled as . . . "schizophrenic" is degraded from full existential and legal status as human agent . . . to someone no longer in possession of his own definition of himself. . . . His time is no longer of his own and the space he occupies is no longer of his choosing. (*The Politics of Experience* 21–22)

Furthermore, the actions that led to this designation of "schizophrenia" and its punitive consequences are the results of conditions that are external to the individual: "In a science of persons, I shall state as axiomatic that: behavior is a function of experience; and both experience and behavior are always in relation to someone or something other than self " (Laing, *The Politics of Experience* 25).

Schizophrenia, according to Laing, although a psychologically crippling condition, does not have its origin within the individual's biochemical makeup.   It develops rather from external conditions and relationships into which individuals enter and against which they respond. This is crucial in Storey's dramas, for those like Arnold Middleton or Richard Fenchurch, characters who have clearly gone mad, are reacting to the external pressures that have shaped their psychic disorders. In other words, it is the intolerable stress upon Arnold Middleton that has produced his behavior—a condition that Laing would identify as wholly external. Moreover, it is society that has labeled such behavior, for want of a better term, as "schizophrenic," a convenient political label that can legally deprive such people of their freedom. The defining element in Laing's definition is pure political power. The application of the term "mad" depends upon who possesses power in a particular situation: the ones defining sanity and insanity and subsequently treating (and possibly punishing through hospitalization or incarceration) those designated as insane.

This, of course, is not to deny that those designated as "mad" do not act in inappropriate ways. They may very well be, as Arnold certainly is, dangerous to himself as well as to others. But Laing argues that the identifiers of the mad—family members and the psychiatrists acting in their behalf—may very well be as mad as or even madder than the certified ones themselves. In addition, they may even be more dangerous to themselves and to society:

When I certify someone insane, I am not equivocating when I write that he is of unsound mind, may be dangerous to himself and others. . . . However, at the same time, I am also aware . . . there are other people who are regarded as sane . . . who may be equally or more dangerous to themselves and others and whom society does not regard as psychotic and fit persons to be in a madhouse. I am aware that . . . the cracked mind of the schizophrenic may *let in* light which does not enter the intact minds of many sane people. (*The Divided Self* 27)

We have in Laing's view a world where there is acceptable madness and unacceptable madness. Moreover, those deemed unacceptably mad may in fact possess important truths, qualities of "light," denied to the very people who have designated them as mad. Arnold Middleton may be in possession of genuine wisdom, but such wisdom must be compromised and repressed in order for the Arnold Middletons of the world to reenter society as functioning individuals.

Laing devotes an entire chapter on the "transcendental experience" associated with psychosis (*Politics of Experience* 131–45). Basically, Laing postulates that "Sanity today appears to rest . . . on a capacity to adapt to the external world—the interpersonal world, and the realm of human collectivities" (141). Moreover, the "external world," the world based upon our "*egoic experience* " (Laing's emphasis), is fraught with "illusion . . . a state of sleep . . . of socially accepted madness" (138). Fortunately there is also an "inner" world that Laing claims provides us with a "way of seeing the external world and all those realities that have no 'external,' 'objective' presence—imagination, dreams, fantasies, trances, the realities of contemplative and meditative states, realities of which modern man, for the most part, has not the slightest direct awareness" (140). However, "the external world is . . . estranged from the inner" and this estrangement produces "a state of darkness" (141–42). Laing believes that a number of "psychotic people" have "transcendental experiences" that enable them to enter the inner world (137) and in so doing to experience themselves in a manner that is not "egoic"—that is to say, in a manner liberated from the rigid perception of "a me-here over against a you-there, within a framework of certain ground structures of space and time shared with other members of society" (137). The crucial distinction here is that although such individuals may be "mad," they are not "ill." Laing writes that the psychotic "experience that a person may be absorbed in, while to others . . . appears simply ill-mad, may be for him veritable manna from heaven" (138).

In his conclusion to his analysis, Laing claims that "true sanity" incorporates the "dissolution of the normal ego," that which is structured within the coordinates of the external world, and the "emergence of the 'inner' archetypal mediators of divine power" (145). The ego must go through a "death and a rebirth" that produces a "new kind of ego-functioning" (145).[7] In "true sanity" the ego would mediate between the external and internal worlds. Such individuals, the "truly sane," would be liberated from the "normal ego" that results in a "false self competently adjusted to our alienated social reality" (144).

As a playwright, Storey provides us dramatically with the experience that Laing is identifying. Madness is not an illness, but a behavioral expression of intolerable conditions and destructive human relationships. The experience examined in *The Restoration of Arnold Middleton* is the extreme isolation of Arnold Middleton, the central character, a young man who appears lost in his own painful solitude and is profoundly unable to connect openly, directly, and honestly with those around him, like his wife, his mother-in-law, his colleagues, and his students.[8] Coupled with this loneliness, Arnold further struggles, and again unsuccessfully, with the psychologically destructive effects of sexual repression, a devastating human experience, which engaged Storey in two novels that he published prior to the production of *The Restoration of Arnold Middleton* (1966): *Flight into Camden* (1960) and *Radcliffe* (1963).[9] In these works, all set in Yorkshire, in the north of England, an area of intense puritanical influence (Stinson 131–43), Storey's principal characters are psychologically injured by the crippling restrictions imposed upon their behavior and sexuality. These restrictions all stem from the puritanical conception of self, a deep disgust with one's own flesh, and the powerful urges that drive human sexuality. Storey defines in *Radcliffe* what he means by "puritanism." John Radcliffe, the father of the hero, Leonard, asks his brother Austen, the novel's most intelligent and sophisticated character (quite possibly Storey's alter ego), what "puritan" actually means, and he is told quite explicitly:

> To have to stoop to something so physical in order to propagate oneself in God's likeness, or any likeness at all, is the one indignity a puritan can scarcely tolerate. They are physically vulnerable—that's what puritans hate. . . . They despise their bodies. (28)[10]

Arnold Middleton, despite his wit and flamboyance, is very much the puritan in the manner that Storey has defined—a "physically vulnerable" young man who cannot deal, as we shall see, with the powerful urges of his own sexuality.

The Restoration of Arnold Middleton is a conventionally written three-act play that to some critics appears as a superbly crafted comedy (Hutchings, *The Plays* 57). One critic even argues that the comedic elements of the play must be read intertextually to appreciate the full dimension of its parody and the range of its humor, and sees Arnold, who has purchased a suit of armor, as none other than "a sort of modern-day British Don Quixote" (Hutchings, *Casebook* 174–76). Michael Billington draws attention in a first-night review to the humor in the play, but he at least does so by balancing the humor against the darker elements in Storey's drama ("First Nights" 30). There is, however, no question that *The Restoration of Arnold Middleton* is funny, but the play is most certainly not a comedy, for its humor covers corrosively tragic events. The humor much more closely approaches the wild comedic elements in modern tragicomedy,[11] for Arnold is clearly a character about whom we will "laugh with one eye and weep with the other" (Guthke 59).[12]

After all, Arnold's plight, despite his sharp wit and his verbal ingenuity, is tragic: he is going insane and, as we shall see, is probably contemplating suicide. In the very first act, it is clearly established that there have been serious sexual problems between Arnold and his wife. In one clue after another, each introduced rather obliquely, since neither Arnold nor his wife will openly confront each other, we discover that Arnold has probably stopped sleeping with his wife and is now craving other women, including, but certainly not limited to, his mother-in-law.[13] Of course this leads Joan, Arnold's wife, into a curiously inappropriate and, at times, explosively humorous display of jealousy toward her own mother, Mrs. Edie Ellis, a woman described by Storey as "a rather unconsciously sensual woman in her late fifties" (1). The jealousy is often expressed over relatively trivial events occurring on the stage and may not at first communicate the seriousness of what is actually going on between Arnold and his wife. For example, early in the first scene, Joan reprimands her mother rather sharply for wearing a suggestive pinafore:

JOAN. I don't like this. I don't.
MRS. ELLIS. What?
JOAN. This! This! (*She grabs and tugs at her mother's pinafore*)
MRS. ELLIS. What?
(*Joan does not answer*)
What's the matter with . . .
JOAN (*moving down L*). It's all wrong!
(*For a moment neither of them can speak*)
MRS. ELLIS. I'll take mine off then.
JOAN. Take *yours* off?
(*Mrs. Ellis takes her apron off slowly; she lays the petite-looking thing absent-mindedly on Arnie's raincoat on the sofa*)
Not there! Not there! (*She snatches it up and throws it on the floor*)
MRS. ELLIS. Joannie . . .
JOAN. I don't like this. I don't.

MRS. ELLIS. What is it, pet?
JOAN. Don't *pet* me. (10–11)

This curious burst of passion between a mother and her daughter is initially quite mystifying and may at first be attributed to Joan's excessive interest in domestic tidiness. As the tension between husband and wife escalates, however, Joan's irrational behavior toward her mother is clearly seen as an expression of the younger woman's jealousy. What is obviously so disturbing to Joan in her mother's innocent discarding of the "petite" pinafore is that it lands on "Arnie's raincoat," suggesting physical contact between mother-in-law and son-in-law, and indeed foreshadowing their subsequent sexual encounter.

Of course, not all the encounters are so seemingly innocent as the casual discarding of a pinafore. Indeed the stakes between daughter and mother are considerably raised as Joan's jealousy is whetted by more sexually obvious and explicit confrontations between herself and her husband. Numerous incidents can be cited in the first act of the play, but a few here will suffice: Joan does not want her mother to accompany her and Arnold that evening to the movies, despite Mrs. Ellis's obvious desire to do so (13); Joan is angered when she is addressed as "Edie," her mother's name, by Arnold (14); and finally Joan, who is dancing with Arnold, forces him, after all three have spent the evening out and are slightly drunk, to choose whether she or her mother has the better legs. Initially this appears quite humorous, but it rapidly turns serious, exposing corrosive feelings within Arnie and intense jealousy verging on rage in his wife:

ARNIE. Edie! She's got the best legs. All the way.
JOAN. (*letting go of Arnie*) What? (*She hiccups*)
ARNIE. Edie's! Edie's all the way.
JOAN. You prefer her to me!

ARNIE. Completely. (*He remains still kneeling, clutching his head, still humored, considering how best to take his revenge*)
JOAN (*with a hiccup*) You don't love *me* !
ARNIE. No!
JOAN. You've never loved me!
ARNIE. Never!
JOAN. You just wanted that (*She hiccups*) and then it was all over.
ARNIE. Absolutely.
JOAN. You don't love me. (20)

Of course, all have drunk too much and the scene is quite funny, for we perhaps assume incorrectly that this is a ludicrous family quarrel with its humor derived from the inappropriateness of a daughter's sexual jealousy so openly expressed toward her own mother. Arnold as well does not appear serious—he seems to be caught up in the frivolity of the exchange, the headiness of the evening, enjoying the merriment in what appears to be his absurd encounter with his wife every bit as much as the audience is apparently enjoying the same ludicrous confrontation. But Arnold is telling the truth in the only way he is capable of telling the truth—through banter, wit, indirection, and oblique reference, the truthfulness of which can later be called into question by his inebriation.

Moreover, the jealousy boiling into rage that is displayed by Joan is equally authentic. Mrs. Ellis senses the impending danger and intervenes quickly, hoping to calm her daughter and her son-in-law and to put an end to the difficult evening.

MRS. ELLIS. (*chastened*) Let's get to bed. For goodness' sake. We're not in our senses. Come on. Let's get up.
JOAN. (*moving down* R) Yes. Yes! I know—I know . . .
MRS. ELLIS. Joan . . .
    (*Joan hiccups*)
ARNIE. (*rising*). Make way! Make way! Move back!
JOAN. You've never loved me. (20)

Joan now actually demands that her mother be sent away: "Arnie. ... Tell her to go." In response, and typical of his inability to be direct, Arnold recites the opening stanza of Blake's "Tiger" with an interesting embellishment on the last two lines:

> Tiger, tiger, burning bright,
> In the forests of the night:
> If you see a five-pound note
> Then take my tip and cut your
> throat.[14]

Joan, understandably, is not placated by Arnold's recitation and continues to insist that her mother be evicted from their home, while her mother, in turn, continues to insist that she be permitted to remain. This develops into a confrontation between Joan and her mother, the latter refusing to leave her daughter and son-in-law's home (21). Arnold again responds flippantly in doggerel and departs, "slamming the door" behind him and leaving his wife and mother-in-law to resolve the painful issue of the jealousy that has now emerged between them (22).

Arnold's sexual desires have not only been expressed toward Mrs. Ellis, but he has obviously been sending out signals to the students in his school as well. When questioned by his mother-in-law about his possible dismissal for allegedly abusing a student, Arnold responds with his typical cynical detachment:

ARNIE. No such fortune for me. (*He sits down on the sofa and begins to tug off his shoes. His mood changes again, and becomes reflective*) If I rape two, or perhaps it may have to be three, I might be asked if I'd mind being moved to another school. But chances of promotion like that are increasingly rare. (*He gets his last shoe off with a struggle*) Rape apart, it's all a question of dead men's shoes, Edie. (6)

Arnold's speech sounds very much like the usual witty diatribe against the bureaucracy of the school system, where any form of incompetence on the part of the staff is tolerated. However, there is evidence in the play to suggest that Arnold has been expressing his sexual needs to his students. Of course, consistent with his style of indirection, Arnold would not openly solicit a student, but he has apparently provoked interest nonetheless. This revelation is demonstrated in the play through the activities of Sheila O'Connor, a student at Arnold's school, whom we first assume is simply a young schoolgirl following her history master home at a distance of "twenty five yards behind" (10) because of an innocent infatuation (9).

However, Sheila O'Connor is employed in this drama because she is initially so easily dismissed as an innocent. Later, at the party arranged by Arnold to assist his friend Hanson in his planned seduction of a fellow teacher, Maureen, Sheila sharply exposes Arnold and identifies the source of his rage—a rage that causes Arnold to abuse Hanson verbally:

ARNIE. Your thoughts, Hanson—they're superfluous here. . . . You've been revealed as a pompous boor. Your otiose circumlocutions no longer sufficient to conceal the cringing, shivering coward within; your boldest gestures about as revelationary as a flea's. . . . (49)

Hanson is verbose and a trifle pompous, a stereotypical English schoolmaster, but nothing he has done warrants the verbal abuse as well as the seriously menacing episode with the Lee-Enfield rifle. Arnold aims the rifle at Hanson and pulls the trigger, and although the weapon is without a firing pin—a fact only subsequently disclosed to calm Hanson's justifiable rage—it is loaded (49). However, it is clearly Hanson's success with Maureen as well as his apparent success with Sheila—the latter now diverting her attention away from Arnold and toward

Hanson (39)—that spurs Arnold into the fierce abuse of his friend. And the only one in the room who correctly identifies the source of Arnold's vehemence is Sheila, young and innocent, but capable of perceiving what is actually occurring and courageous enough to express herself[15]:

SHEILA. It's because he's [Arnold] jealous. That's why he's gone . . .
MAUREEN (*rising*) Sheila!
SHEILA. He is. He's jealous of Mr. Hanson. Anybody can see.
   (*Joan is more disillusioned than annoyed*)
JOAN (*passively*) Oh, for goodness' sake. (*Moving to L. of Maureen*) Get her out. . .
SHEILA. He is! You're all jealous. All of you. (50–51)

Shortly after this confrontation, Arnold seduces Edie, his mother-in-law; and it is Edie who, drunk, disheveled, and "dressed in men's pyjamas," informs her daughter of the incestuous incident (53).[16] When later confronted by his wife, Arnold, who can never be direct, employs a dark humor, claiming that now he will "do the only decent thing" and "marry" his mother-in-law (58). To his wife's suggestion that he leave the house, Arnold resists, suggesting that he will go "mad" instead:

ARNIE . . . Perhaps I could go mad. Insanity, you know, is the one refuge I've always felt I was able to afford. (58)

Arnold retreats from those around him. He is no longer teaching or even seeing people and dismisses Edie completely, pretending that she no longer even exists physically (66). The house, in the interim, under Joan's supervision, has been thoroughly cleaned and tidied up, and all the artifacts, save the sword that came with the suit of armor, have been deposited in the outside trash bins (59–61). In the final scene, Arnold, visited by Hanson and Maureen, has moved completely over the edge, and, now a towel wrapped turban-like around his head, he carries his sword (61)[17] and speaks passionately in honor of royalty:

ARNIE. Goodness and kings. (*He studies Hanson a moment*) Kings rise above themselves. They become—inanimate. Formed. (*He shapes it with his hands, then looks around at them*) Do you know what the greatest threat to the present century is? (*He pauses*) The pygmies. (*He smiles at them*) (65)

Finally, alone with his wife, Arnold devotes himself to his recovery. He will go back to school and reintegrate himself into his life. He will, in Laingian terms, reenter the "external world" and function in a socially acceptable manner. To further emphasize the sudden return of his sanity, Storey has Arnold engage in what appears to be a primal scream that functions as an exorcism cleansing him of his madness:

ARNIE. Rest. Recuperation. Work!
JOAN. Yes.
    (*There is a moment's silence. Joan moves C*)
ARNIE (suddenly, crying out) Oh!
JOAN. Arnie!
ARNIE. Oh! There's something coming out!
JOAN. Arnie—it's all right. (70)

The exchange continues as Joan encourages Arnie to face whatever darkness is within him. Finally, Arnie releases the demons within:

ARNIE. Oh. NOW! (*He screams, hugely*)
    (*There is a moment's silence*)
JOAN. It's all over. (70)

Presumably we are now expected to believe that Arnie has successfully worked through his crippling behavior and the restoration towards health has begun:

JOAN. Are you coming up?
ARNIE. Up?
JOAN. Yes.
ARNIE. Have I finished? (*He looks around*)
JOAN. Yes.
ARNIE. I've finished?
JOAN. I think so.
ARNIE. Are you sure?
JOAN. Yes.
ARNIE. Oh. Oh. Oh. Joan.
    Oh. Joan.
        Thank God. The LIGHTS fade to a Blackout, as—the Curtain
falls.   (70)

Arnold's wife may be convinced that the madness has departed, but there is very little reason for us to believe so, notwithstanding the dramatic shout for sanity. Indeed, it is hard to believe that this man will return to his teaching or that his marriage will be saved.[18] One of the serious problems in the play is that Storey does not deal adequately and truthfully with the consequences of the seduction of the mother-in-law[19];   the act is only vaguely hinted at and even a close and perceptive reader like Ruby Cohn is not absolutely certain the seduction took place: "There remains . . . a fissure in Arnie's mind, which seems to be associated with his mother-in-law, whom he has perhaps seduced, and whose existence he has started to deny" (Hutchings, *Casebook* 80).
    Arnold has indeed seduced his mother-in-law, but what has not taken place is Arnold's restoration, despite the glib reassurances of his wife. Storey has not dealt fully with the act of seduction and examined its ramifications. It seems, almost, to pass unnoticed by Joan, Arnold's wife

and Edie's daughter.   She certainly would have been
much more deeply affected by her husband's incestuous
conduct with her own mother, and her reassuring presence at the end appears, at the very least, profoundly
disingenuous.   Arnold's seduction of his mother-in-law
also forces Edie out of the house to live on her own and
the serious consequences of this event are not fully explored in the play as well.   Storey treats these actions with
almost the same indirection and verbal wit that Arnold
employs when confronted about his own behavior.

From the perspective of Laingian psychology, Arnold
has gone mad, but paradoxically he is not sick.[20]   His behavior is clearly inappropriate, to say the very least, and
his careless conduct with the Lee-Enfield rifle and the
sword suggests potentially dangerous behavior—toward
others as well as himself.   However, as Laing has argued,
such schizophrenic "behavior is a function of experience";
the designation, "schizophrenic," moreover,   is a
"political event," not an appropriate medical designation
(*The Politics of Experience* 25).   Arnold is reacting to the
complex stress of intolerable, external conditions. [21]

However, Arnold's restoration remains unconvincing.
Indeed, in a Laingian sense, the conditions of his life
within his environment—his employment and marriage—do not change.   As a result, his "experience" of life
is unaffected and this experience is the very source of the
powerful stress afflicting him.   Nor does Arnold anywhere in the play ever confront these conditions with a
minimum of honesty, integrity, and courage.   He does
condemn those around him as "pygmies," constituting
"the greatest threat to the present century" (65), but this
speech, delivered as a paean to the loss of royalty, hardly
constitutes insight into his complex and agonizing condition.   In addition, Arnold's incestuous behavior, as well as
his total dismissal of Edie as even a physical presence,

does not provide him with sufficient stature to comment so negatively upon the current level of morality. There is, further, no intuitive jump or Laingian "transcendental moment" on Arnold's part that provides him with insight into his "internal world," so that he can restructure his ego and function more appropriately in the "external world." Moreover, the dialogue between Arnold and Joan at the end (69–70) is disingenuous, and we appear to be in the presence of two characters who have just entered the play—they do not even seem consistent with the Arnold and the Joan who have previously occupied the stage. Arnold's cloyingly dependent behavior toward his wife, as well as his primal scream at the play's conclusion, suggests more of a devastated individual than the witty and acerbic Arnold, however troubled and intimidating, whom we have known (69–70).

One final comment should be made about the suit of armor that initially appears center stage in the play and, although hidden for the most part in a cupboard (3), is constantly referred to in the drama. The suit of armor actually parallels the voyage of Arnold in the play—as he collapses into madness, the armor is ultimately disassembled and placed "in pieces, lying in a pile on sacking between the sofa and the chair" (54). Ultimately it, like the other artifacts, with the exception of the sword, is discarded into trash bins. This disposal of the armor further parallels the possible later disposal of Arnold himself, either through suicide, as was originally intended, or incarceration in a mental institution. This is a perfect example of what Austin Quigley recognizes as "Storey's originality as a dramatist—his ability to transform conventional technical devices into structural images which control the thematic implications of the plays" ("Emblematic Structure" 261). Curiously Quigley does not include the suit of armor in *The Restoration of Arnold Middleton* as

as an example of the "structural images" Storey so successfully employs, but the armor clearly functions in this particular dramatic mode, and it would have been a perfect
example of Storey's transformation of a technical device
into a brilliant structural image had the playwright been
faithful to the tragic fate that awaited Arnold at the play's
conclusion.

As the play now stands, it is both witty and tragic, but a
dramatic failure nonetheless. Arnold's dilemma is not
convincingly resolved in the drama's closing moments.
Perhaps Arnold can be returned to sanity, but that particular restoration does not occur in Storey's play.

Home, produced in 1970, some four years after the initial production of The Restoration of Arnold Middleton,
represents a significant sophistication in terms of Storey's
presentation of madness as well as his developing technique as a dramatist. In The Restoration of Arnold
Middleton the focus was placed upon one individual,
Arnold, as he withdrew and cracked under the stress of external pressure. The drama examined Arnold's descent
into mad behavior, and, however unconvincingly presented, his final restoration. In Home we are presented
with an entire society that at first appears thoroughly sane
and safe. Only slowly do we begin to realize that there is
something terribly wrong with the characters who stroll
and chat so amiably before us on stage. Storey's presentation of madness in this drama is considerably more ambitious and complex. It also represents the work of a much
more sophisticated dramatist whose technique in Home
now represents a broad range of literary influences.

While The Restoration of Arnold Middleton was a
conventionally structured three-act drama, a tragicomedy
clearly within the tradition of contemporary realism,[22]
Home is the work of a dramatist influenced by the naturalism in the plays of Chekhov,[23] as well as the darker,

more fragmented and disorienting dramatic structures created by both Beckett and Pinter.[24]   Carol Rosen identifies Chekhov's influence upon David Storey, particularly in Storey's dramatic use of a "new naturalism [that] results in the creation onstage of a heightened, pervasive reality."   Rosen quotes Chekhov's argument for the important need of this mode of drama:

> The demand is made that the hero and the heroine of a play should be dramatically effective. But in real life people do not shoot themselves, or hang themselves or fall in love . . . every minute. They spend most of their time eating, drinking . . . talking nonsense. It is therefore necessary that this should be shown on the stage. ("Symbolic Naturalism" 277)

We do not have to go very far into *Home* to see Storey's characters engage in the type of everyday "nonsense" demanded by Chekhov.   Harry,[25] a thoroughly respectable middle-aged gentleman, "a specialist in house warming" (43), encourages Jack to look at his newspaper.   Jack, an equally respectable middle-aged gentleman, "a retailer in preserves" (43), who dresses in a more "dandyish" manner (11) and carries an elegant cane (27), is quite responsive to Harry's request.   Both men have run into each other in what is possibly a garden, a park, a resort, or the grounds of some kind of institution like a hospital—we are not at all certain and at this point the playwright is not telling us.   However, Harry has Jack examine the newspaper he has been reading:

HARRY. Seen that? (*Points at the paper.*)
JACK (*reads. Then*). By jove ... (Reads again briefly.) Well . . . you get some surprises . . . Hello . . . (*Reads farther down, turning edge of paper over.*) Good God.
HARRY. What I felt.
JACK. The human mind. (*Shakes his head.*)
HARRY. Oh dear, yes.

JACK. One of these days ...
HARRY. Ah, yes.
JACK. Then where will they be?
HARRY. Oh, yes.
JACK. Never give it a thought.
HARRY. No ... Never.
JACK (*reads again*). By jove ... (*Shakes his head.*) (12)

This is the language of unrelated utterances, of pauses and interjections, of fractured thoughts: it is representative of polite chatter that is hollow, empty of all content, incapable of expressing coherence or even feeling. It is speech for the sake of speaking, and it is, at its most quintessential, simply noise. We, at any rate, have no idea what Harry and Jack are talking about or for that matter what they are examining in the newspaper, and we begin to wonder early on if even they themselves have any idea of what they are ever talking about. For speech, like all activities in *Home*, is produced to get through the day—to pass the time. Jack, who later pairs off with Marjorie, comments to her on the advantage of a meal taken late in the afternoon: "One of the advantages of a late lunch, of course, is that it leaves a shorter space to tea" (66). The problem is dealing with the moment and whatever can fill the spaces of time—nonsensical chatter or a "late lunch"—are employed as devices to stave off the dreariness and the aimlessness of their lives.

If these men, who are most impeccable in their manners, talk to each other at length but never say anything, then indeed their language is stripped clean of its denotative and connotative qualities. Any idea can elicit any other idea, regardless of how irrelevant the two ideas are. This particular exchange echoes a witty interchange in Pinter's "The Dumb Waiter" (1960). Gus and Ben, Pinter's two professional criminals, are vastly different in sensibilities and backgrounds from Storey's characters, but they engage in similar idle chatter, the Chekhovian language of "everyday nonsense" in response to a newspaper story:

BEN. Kaw!
He picks up the paper.
What about this? Listen to this!
He refers to the paper.
A man of eighty-seven wanted to cross the road. But there was a lot of traffic, see? He couldn't see how he was going to squeeze through. So he crawled under the lorry.
GUS. He what?
BEN. He crawled under a lorry. A stationary lorry.
GUS. No?
BEN. The lorry started and ran over him.
GUS. Get away.
BEN. It's enough to make you want to puke, isn't it?
GUS. Who advised him to do a thing like that?
BEN. A man of eighty-seven crawling under a lorry!
GUS. It's unbelievable.
BEN. It's down here in black and white.
GUS. Incredible.
Silence. ("The Dumb Waiter" 129–130)

Unlike Harry and Jack, Ben and Gus do discuss the contents of the article they are reading, but the result is similar in the fragmented discourse that emerges.[26]

Moreover, Pinter's influence upon *Home,* despite Storey's disclaimer (Flatley 1), is pervasive in the manner in which the dialogue in the drama is constructed. Issues are not discussed and discourse is not pursued in a coherent manner. Such examples of Pinteresque rhythm and fragmentation are abundant. Harry and Jack are not actually speaking to each other, but are engaged in an amusing exchange of word associations. Ideas bounce off each other like billiard balls, triggering reactions that produce chains of fragmented speech. Consider the following exchange as Harry examines Jack's cane:

HARRY. You seldom see canes of this quality these days.
JACK. No. No. That's right.
HARRY. I believe they've gone out of fashion.
JACK. They have.
HARRY. Like beards.
JACK. Beards!
HARRY. My father had a small moustache.
JACK. A moustache I've always thought became a man.
HARRY. Chamberlain.
JACK. Roosevelt.
HARRY. Schweitzer.
JACK. Chaplin.
HARRY. Hitler . . .
JACK. Travel, I've always felt, was a great broadener of the mind.
(27)

From "canes of quality" to travel, the dialogue rambles on, and at no point is there even an attempt at sustained, coherent discourse.

Joining Harry and Jack as fellow residents are Kathleen who limps, and Marjorie, who assists her (38). Unlike the two men, who are both exceedingly discreet, the women are very working class[27] and always eager to be as blunt as possible about their feelings and behavior. Kathleen, complaining about her shoes, tells Marjorie how she tried to be admitted into a hospital for a long stay:

KATHLEEN. Cor blimey . . . take these off if I thought I could get 'em on again . . . (Groans.) Tried catching a serious disease.
MARJORIE. When was that?
KATHLEEN. Only had me in two days. Said, nothing the matter with you, my girl.
MARJORIE. Don't believe you.
KATHLEEN. Next thing: got home; smashed everything in sight.
MARJORIE. No?
KATHLEEN. Winders. Cooker . . . Nearly broke me back . . . Thought I'd save the telly. Still owed eighteen months. Thought: 'Everything or nothing, girl.'
MARJORIE: Rotten programmes. (*Takes down umbrella.*) (41)

Again there is a similar exchange, as ideas carom against each other without any particular thought pursued or developed—in this particular exchange, from gaining admission into a hospital to the "Rotten programmes" on television.

Finally there is Alfred[28] who complements the four inmates in an interesting manner. While Jack and Harry as well as Kathleen and Marjorie are perfectly conscious of the fact they are institutionalized—and resort to a variety of rationalizations to explain their situation—Alfred is unaware of where he is. Even in the world of the mad, there are people like Alfred who are undeniably mad— madder than the mad. With Alfred's inclusion in the play, Storey extends the range of human behavior, stretching from the well-mannered gentlemen and coarse ladies to the obviously mad and muscle-bound Alfred, the unfortunate victim of a lobotomy, who enjoys removing chairs and tables, and believes he is "older than his dad" (70). Moreover, Alfred thinks that he is actually at home in the institution to which he has been confined. Marjorie questions Alfred:

MARJORIE. What you in for?
ALFRED. In what?
MARJORIE. Thinks he's at home, he does. . . . (69)

Aside from the Pinteresque rhythms in the dialogue, Samuel Beckett can be identified as the principal influence upon the structure of Storey's play.[29] Ruby Cohn identifies *Home* as "a major work of contemporary English theater" and traces Beckett's influence, particularly in Storey's echoing of *Waiting for Godot* in *Home*'s "symmetrical" structure where the four inmates, Harry and Jack and Marjorie and Kathleen, sustain "inaction over two acts."

Furthermore, both titles, *Waiting for Godot* and *Home,* are enigmatic: the mystery of the awaited presence in one play and the mystery of the designated home in the other" (36–38). As the bleak landscape in *Godot* communicates a disorienting sense of bewilderment, an absence of a localized setting, an absence of a psychological as well as a geographical orientation and grounding, so the territory of *Home* is in fact similarly disorienting and unspecifiable. Storey's comments on the play's setting are significantly terse [30]: "The stage is bare but for a round metalwork table,[31] set slightly off-centre, stage left, and two metalwork chairs" (11). In *The Restoration of Arnold Middleton,* the plot unfolds in a conventional, realistic manner. Most importantly, the focus is upon Arnold and the suspense generated is directed toward his fate: we simply want to know what will happen to him. Will he confront the terror gripping him or will he succumb, falling into insanity and possibly suicide? The plot is conventional as the story proceeds through its three acts, and the behavior of the characters follows certain recognizable psychological sequences of cause and effect, acts that can be analyzed and reasonably understood in terms of the characters' pressing needs.

But no such sequence of discernible action or development occurs in *Home.* There is no plot in the sense of a story with credible characters engaging in forms of behavior, be they rational or irrational, that we can come to understand—or even argue about—through intellectual analysis. There is no central action, like Arnold's steady plunge into insanity, structuring the events of the drama. Furthermore, as *The Restoration of Arnold Middleton* represents the dramatic depiction of the voyage from sanity to madness in a single individual, *Home* represents a society as completely mad, a world where sanity itself is absent. In *Home* there are only the inmates and the world that they have created among themselves. They do not change as a result of pressure or events in their static lives; they simply are, and what they are is mad.

As B. A. Young has observed, there is primarily an extended, linear experience in *Home*, a "heartbreaking" experience to be sure, but an experience, nonetheless, of our witnessing the mad locked into their world of "incommunicability" (72). Consequently "*Home* does not develop but is slowly unveiled as a whole that was whole when the house-lights first went down" (73). It is a drama where the reality of what we are seeing slowly emerges, the pieces fitting together leisurely within the lazy rhythm of the play, a dramatic rhythm punctuated by the characters' frequent lapses of memory, pauses in their speech, and the endless digressions as one character's idea, as we have seen, elicits unrelated ideas from his or her interlocutor, everyone responding within the choppy and bumpy give and take of the dialogue. We are in a very contemporary mode of tragicomedy.

Martin Esslin, for example, in writing about *Waiting for Godot*, has illustrated the manner in which such a play—a play without overt action—operates and communicates its meaning:

In Beckett's *Waiting For Godot* the meaning of the play emerges only when the audience recognises that the second act has the identical structure as the first. The structure itself acts as a signifier to tell the audience what the play has been saying: namely, that it is a metaphor for the unchanging sequence . . . the passing of time, experienced as 'waiting,' the dependence of human beings on each other, the rhythm of meetings and partings. The suspense of a play in which 'nothing happens' here grows from the gradual unfolding of the image. It is the suspense created when we watch the gradual unfolding of a flower. What holds our attention here is the unfolding, step by step, of a pre-existing pattern. The question in such a dramatic structure is not primarily:

what is going to happen next?[32]   But simply: what is happening?
What image is here being unfolded?   (*The Field of Drama* 120–121)

Of course, Esslin could have been writing about *Home*
as well as *Waiting for Godot,* so close structurally are the
two works. Clearly, Beckett's influence on the structure of
Home is pervasive, and we feel ourselves in the presence
of a space that cannot be specifically located and with
characters who are essentially unknowable. Furthermore,
Home exhibits a closeness, structurally, to Beckett's
Endgame, a play with clear eschatological concerns that
are echoed repeatedly in Storey's drama. In this specific
critical context, Carol Rosen has identified *Home* and
Endgame, among other works, as models of contemporary
plays of "impasse," works in which characters are trapped
not only physically within an institution like a prison or
an insane asylum, but also within the developing awareness that their situation admits of no solution, for the
world beyond their physical barriers, should release ever
occur, is itself corrupt, a world empty of moral significance
and sustaining value (*Plays of Impasse* 3–24, 128–45, 268–
78).

Not only is the world—the sane world—beyond the
edge of the characters' physical existence in *Home*   vapid
and deceitful, it is also dangerous, having promoted for
each of the characters the web of circumstances that has
produced their inappropriate behavior—or, as Laing
would admit, their insanity.   However, such individuals
are not sick. "No one *has* [Laing's emphasis] schizophrenia, like having a cold. . . . He is schizophrenic" (*The
Divided Self* 34). For example, as Laing observes, an individual who claims that "he is an unreal man or that he
is dead in all seriousness" is in fact expressing his
"existence as he experiences it" and that "experience is insanity" (*The Divided Self* 38); and we must interpret such

behavior "as expressive of . . . existence" (*The Divided Self* 31). In Alfred's case, the so-called sane world has also produced injuries inside the institution by removing part of his brain through an unfortunate lobotomy with obvious disastrous consequences.[33]

But on an even darker note, the sane world beyond is ultimately perceived by Harry and Jack as sinister and dangerous—a sense of an almost growing apocalyptic eruption begins to threaten even the tiny patch of earth that provides Harry and Jack with shelter and protection. Harry and Jack frequently refer to England as the little island that brought civilization to the world (19, 22, 79), but the historical situation is changing profoundly and rapidly. Now there is fear that this "island itself might very well be flooded" (28) and over England "This little island. . . . The sun has set" (78).[34] Slowly, there is the identification of the grounds of the home with England itself and the world beyond the institution as producing a situation of cataclysmic menace. This is demonstrated in the ending to Storey's drama where we find Jack and Harry alone on stage, as the various pieces of furniture around them are removed systematically by Alfred. In a clever stroke of dramatic irony, the insane asylum is seen at the end as providing a haven, albeit a temporary one, from the deteriorating conditions of present day England:

JACK. Empire the like of which no one has ever seen.
HARRY. No. My word.
JACK. Light of the world.
HARRY. Oh, yes.
JACK. Penicillin.
HARRY. Penicillin.
JACK. Darwin.
HARRY. Darwin.
JACK. Newton.
HARRY. Newton.

JACK. Milton.
HARRY. My word.
JACK. Sir Walter Raleigh.
HARRY. Goodness. Sir . . .
JACK. Lost his head.
HARRY. Oh, yes. (*Rises; comes downstage.*)
JACK. This little island.
HARRY. Shan't see its like.
JACK. Oh, no.
HARRY. The sun has set. (79)

England's scientific and artistic brilliance, represented by luminaries in science, the arts, and adventure, became humanity's "light"; the two men proceed, however, in a chronologically retrograde order, from Sir Alexander Fleming, the discoverer of penicillin in 1928, to the courtier, writer, and adventurer, Sir Walter Raleigh who "lost his head" in 1618. There is something darkly appropriate in this reverse presentation of glory, for as one great man, Sir Walter Raleigh, was beheaded, through, to many, an act of treachery, so England itself will face its cultural decapitation—that is to say, its scientific and artistic light will no longer provide benefits to humanity.

Alfred removes the remaining chairs, leaving the stage appropriately bare, as Jack and Harry continue in their dirge, not only for England, but for the entire world, for they now comment that the very creation itself was a "mistake" (82) and it will not happen again. Here Storey communicates the darkest of all cosmological visions: there will be no renewal after the world is destroyed. Quite simply, and quite tragically, mankind was a mistake.

HARRY. See the church.
(*They gaze off*)
JACK. Shouldn't wonder He's disappointed. (Looks up)
HARRY. Oh, yes.
JACK. Heart-break.

HARRY. Oh, yes.
JACK. Same mistake . . . Won't make it twice.
HARRY. Oh, no.
JACK. Once over. Never again. (82)

Now Jack and Harry are alone on the empty and bleak stage, a setting curiously appropriate to their observation that even God himself will no longer have anything to do with his creation. Storey's use of space here is effectively united with his theme of impending cosmological disaster. William Free notes an interesting difference between Storey and Pinter in their use of stage space: in Pinter "the tensions from outside press in" whereas in Storey the tensions flow outward ("Ironic Anger" 315). As the two men, Jack and Harry, stare outward the whole glory of English history collapses in the face of an impending cataclysmic eruption. Outside, beyond the stage, in the consciousness of these two men, is the presence of the future, and it is a very dark and dangerous presence indeed. Not only is the past and the present over, but time itself will be extinguished: there will be no future, and there will be no second chance. A profound solitude has settled on the two men as Jack, who once wanted to be a priest (16), notes that "He's disappointed" and will not make the same mistake twice. As both men cry, the lights go to darkness while the fullness of Storey's profoundly bleak vision is dramatically conveyed.

R. D. Laing has defined the distinction between the "absence of relationships" and the darker existential "experience of every relationship as an absence" which is the difference between "loneliness," a relatively benign phenomenon, and "perpetual solitude," a condition of "permanent despair" (*The Politics of Experience* 37).

In his drama, Storey has isolated this "perpetual solitude" within Jack and Harry as they gaze out into space—as, in fact, they gaze at us, the audience, the supposedly

sane world confronting them. As we observe them we
perhaps see in their reflection our own perplexities and
weaknesses, for what has been demonstrated here, in ac-
cord with Laing's theories, is the thin, almost imperceptible line that separates those on the inside from those on
the outside. At any rate, both Harry and Jack are locked
within themselves and each sees no hope of ever again
making a human connection. They are apparently awaiting a devastation—England will be flooded (28)—and
there is, as we have seen, no hope that the world can experience a renewal. It is the bleakest possible vision as
well as the most tragic. And it is a very powerful play and
one of Storey's finest.

Sisters (1978) further extends Storey's handling and
understanding of the complexity of madness. As *The
Restoration of Arnold Middleton* identified the family as
the agent that often produces madness through the intolerable stress it generates, so *Sisters* examines the false
sense of haven and security that the family represents.
Here, of course, R. D. Laing would agree, as he himself
cautions us to think of the "schizophrenogenic" conditions of the family itself (*The Divided Self* 190). Yet it is
to the family that Adrienne returns for succor and support. In Laingian terms, she returns to the very source of
her madness, initially unaware of the duplicitous danger
that awaits her. If Adrienne learns a lesson in *Sisters*, it is
simply that the source of her pathology is the very family
to which she has returned for support and healing.

Moreover, *Sisters*, like *Home*, extends Storey's capacity
to dramatize the illusive and deceptive qualities of the
mad. As in *Home*, what we are seeing is actually different
from what is actually there. In the earlier play, we as-
sumed that the world before us was quite sane before the
realization occurred that we were in the presence of mad
residents of a mental institution; in *Sisters* we completely

confuse the situation between Adrienne, who initially appears innocent and quite sane, and the members of her sister's household, a brothel, who appear manipulative and deceptive. As the play develops, it is not only Adrienne's madness that is discovered but also her capacity to manipulate and to control events. It is a play where the apparently innocent one suddenly turns, and our perception of those on stage is radically altered.

Sisters was produced at the Royal Exchange Theatre in Manchester in 1978 and was never moved onto a London stage—nor, for that matter, was it ever produced in New York.[35] This is a serious omission, for *Sisters* is a play deserving of a first-rate professional production and far more serious critical and scholarly attention than it has apparently received.[36]

Initially we are led to believe that Adrienne has been victimized by unfortunate past experiences. However, there are numerous clues in the play that suggest Adrienne seriously misrepresents the events of her life, as she lies quite convincingly about the husband who left her (102) and the baby who fell victim to a miscarriage (99). At the same time, she sounds quite credible in expressing her need to flee from her parental home because of its "mediocrity" and the "sickening people with . . . their sickening, stifling self-righteousness" (72).[37]

Finally, we learn that Adrienne is herself mad and about to be returned to the institution from which she has fled. However, her behavior, like that of the two gentlemen in *Home*, initially appears quite sane and even wholesome, particularly in contrast to the bizarre environment she discovers in her sister's home.

At first Adrienne represents an enviable example of human resilience and commitment—a willingness to struggle regardless of the serious and even tragic consequences of past misfortunes. The setting of the play, however, suggests the persistence of trouble. For Adrienne, who assumes that she has arrived at a safe haven, Carol's home, has in fact arrived at a brothel. Considering her unhappiness and vulnerability as well as an absence of any supportive connection with her family during the years when she had left home—she had not even attended the funerals of her mother and father (68, 69) nor had she even seen her sister Carol in seven years (82)—we have considerable reason to fear for her safety.

To further complicate matters and to ensure a rich level of dramatic irony, the identity of the brothel is intentionally hidden from Adrienne. She is not immediately conscious [38] of what in fact is occurring in Carol's home.[39] Actually, Adrienne was expected to arrive on a day when Carol had not planned any "appointments" (105). However, she arrives a day early and inadvertently walks in on the brothel while it is in operation. Since the other inhabitants of the brothel have no idea who she is—Carol never discussed her sister, not even with Mrs. Donaldson, her surrogate mother (62)—the assumption on the part of the others is that Adrienne has arrived home to work with her sister as a prostitute.[40] Police Constable Crawford, who is one of Storey's funniest creations, a character of almost Dickensian dimensions,[41] displays sexual interest in Adrienne and even returns on the following day hoping to establish a working sexual liaison, as he is apparently losing interest in the prostitutes whom he has been visiting:

ADRIENNE: I'll be around, I think, for quite some time.
CRAWFORD: Right. I'll look forward to that. (*Confidentially*) The material around here isn't all to my liking as a matter of fact. A change of ingredients wouldn't go astray. (144)

Because of Adrienne's apparent naiveté and the relative discretion of those around her, she continues to appear unaware of what is actually occurring between the prostitutes and their guests—although Police Constable Crawford, with his usual bluntness, observes: "If she's [Adrienne] living in a knocking-shop, I think somebody ought to tell her" (105). However, we discover that Adrienne has never been married (138); that she apparently attempted suicide (140); and that she has just escaped from a mental institution to which, at the end of the play, in a scene reminiscent of the tragic end of Williams's *A Streetcar Named Desire* (1947), she is forcefully returned (147–148). Furthermore, as the activities of the brothel appear to be misunderstood by Adrienne, her activities appear to be equally misunderstood by the other characters in the brothel. Initially, she is depicted as an innocent victim of the activities of those around her, but those around her are equally innocent of her activities. Storey has the dramatic irony cut both ways: she has been manipulating her environment in order to establish a certain leverage of power and control, as the environment has been manipulating her. She is, in fact, trying to assume a measure of control over the very establishment whose function is being intentionally concealed from her. After establishing the true nature of what is going on in her sister's home, Adrienne negotiates for a partnership with Tom, her sister's husband, the pimp and the owner of the brothel:

ADRIENNE: How much would you want?
TOM: For what?
ADRIENNE (*flinching*): To take half of what you earn. (127)

Obviously, Adrienne's mask of innocence and vulnerability is a clever dramatic presence with which to explore the complexity of the reality created on stage—who is actually there and what is actually there; and, more importantly, in the context of this particular play, who is actually manipulating whom.   Storey achieves the realization that Adrienne is mad slowly, as the evidence of her past troubles mount, and, in a particularly witty as well as chilling scene, he permits Adrienne to reveal herself.[42]   In a confrontation with Constable Crawford, Adrienne points out that when she lived with her family in a world without "vision" and "dreams," she "lavished" all her affection on Carol.   In disgust at this "common" life, she fled to make her "fortune," but just at the moment when true freedom was at hand she gave birth to a "baby."

CRAWFORD: (*pause. Then*): You should have aborted it.
ADRIENNE: I couldn't kill a living thing.
CRAWFORD: It's not living.
ADRIENNE: Isn't it?
CRAWFORD: Not for a while. Tha's two or three months you know when tha could have got rid of it.
ADRIENNE: It's extraordinary . . . it's what my husband said . . . I thought I should save it . . . I thought, you see, it might be like Jesus.
   (CRAWFORD *gazes at her.*)
ADRIENNE: I said, 'Suppose it's like the Second Coming.'
CRAWFORD (pause): I don't understand.
ADRIENNE: Suppose it was Christ. Suppose Mary had had a child: suppose the second Mary had had an abortion. (102)

Crawford may be, as he claims, a superb police officer with "automatic recall" (97), but he has no talent at spotting megalomania and madness.   With his typical lack of understanding, he comments on the possible consequences if Adrienne had had an abortion:

CRAWFORD: I see what you mean. We're all waiting here for a new Messiah and the bastards went and aborted him. . . . (102)

But Storey's play unfortunately bogs down early on in excessively expositional dialogue [43] and at least one highly improbable event. We are expected to believe that Adrienne, who flees from the mental hospital in the middle of the night, actually takes with her a heavy trunk—in fact, a trunk so heavy that both Tom, a muscular ex-footballer, and the driver of Adrienne's taxi are unable to carry it up one flight of stairs to her room. It will have to remain where it is sitting in the hall (126).[44]

Most importantly, however, Carol, who is a principal character in the drama, is much too thinly drawn and too curiously disingenuous to preserve the intense interest in her relationship with Adrienne, and this relationship between the two sisters is central to the drama.

Lois Overbeck notes that women in Storey's works, even if they are of central importance, as they obviously are in *Sisters*, have no power in defining the roles they assume in life. Such roles are determined by men (Hutchings, *Casebook* 163). Carol's life, consequently, despite her intelligence and decency, is prescribed within the limits set by her rather brutal "boozer" of a husband, Tom, for whom she works as a prostitute in the hopes of someday reforming him:

CAROL: I live with Tom. I'm trying to change him. I'm trying to drag him out of this mess. I want to salvage something from it.
ADRIENNE: He doesn't want to change.
CAROL: No one wants to change, my love. You have to change: and by you changing they change also. You have to educate them, Aid. He was brought up in a world of opportunists, of grabbing what you can, by measuring your life by what you've achieved. I want him to change: I want him to be able to lose all that. You talking to him like that isn't going to help me much. (137)

This observation on Carol's part is as difficult to believe as is the presence of the heavy trunk that Adrienne carried on her back as she fled in the night. It is of course a much more serious defect in the drama: Carol cannot be serious in this peculiar admission. Her husband does not work and is a pimp, living off the wages of the prostitutes in his house, including his own wife. He is brutal, often physically harming Carol, even while she's pregnant (134), and has in fact had a sexual encounter with Adrienne that Carol now knows about (139). Yet Carol chooses to define herself in the role of a savior regardless of the devastating consequences such a mission entails.

Her preaching about her commitment to personal change, and, in changing herself, changing Tom, is pompous and disingenuous. Of course, such a commitment is possible, not only in drama but in real life, as destructive relationships certainly exist and, conceivably, can be mended. The problem in *Sisters*, however, is Carol. She appears as one without feeling, without emotion, without passion. Her treachery at the end of the drama has no impact. Obviously, Carol notifies the home to send a car for Adrienne who most desperately fights to preserve her freedom (145–48). But Adrienne is betrayed, not by her sister, but by a nonentity.

In this respect, Carol is similar to Joan in *The Restoration of Arnold Middleton*. Both women exist solely in their cold and lifeless subservience to their husbands: Joan's devotion and reassurances are supposed to restore mad Arnold to sanity, although we see him, at the end, as considerably more lobotomized than sane (70); Carol's devotion to a thoroughly cruel and vicious man is supposed to rescue him at some future date, although we do not even see minimal evidence that this is possible. Tom remains Tom—a self-consumed, violent egoist, who spends his time in the local pub and is bitterly convinced that his first wife ruined his life and prevented him from becoming a football "star" (121).[45]

But it is Carol herself that seriously weakens this otherwise fine play. Had Storey created two women instead of one, the ending of this drama would indeed have been quite tragic. We would not only feel Adrienne's loss, but we would also feel Carol's treachery, as well as the sharp pain that is involved in betrayal—for she has, however we may seek to justify the act, betrayed her sister—and this unfortunately does not occur.

In one sense, Adrienne's experiences have penetrated into the mythology of the family as the place to return to for security and support. Storey's play demonstrates R. D. Laing's observation that the family itself is treacherous and can produce madness (*The Divided Self* 189–90). The family, Adrienne tells her sister, is not really there. It is a mirage. It is deceptive, as Adrienne points out, before being forcefully returned to the institution from which she had fled: "Families are an illusion, Carol. You have to destroy them to stay alive" (147).

Stages (1992), Storey's most recent drama, is his most complex and ambitious treatment of madness. It is a play of recall [46] of the particular stages in Richard Fenchurch's life; and, like Storey himself, the protagonist is a novelist and a painter, as well as an ex-erector of tents (193) and the son of a coal miner (201). These stages, so to speak, are steps in a descent that have led inexorably to Fenchurch's loneliness and madness in the undisclosed town where he is presently living. As such, of all Storey's plays this is the most graphic depiction of madness on the stage. Storey is not, as in his previous works, representing madness for our observation and understanding. In *Stages*, particularly in the drama's poetic conclusion, we are drawn close to madness as a necessary mode of survival, and, in a Laingian analysis, as an expression of "existence" (*The Divided Self* 31). Fenchurch's madness is what enables him to survive and, as we shall see, expresses the intolerable conditions of his existence.

Structurally, the play is a series of dialogues between Richard Fenchurch and those, like his daughter Karen, who have come in an attempt to rescue him from his loneliness and his eccentric behavior that others in the town have noted with alarm (192). But the dialogues slowly change, almost imperceptibly, into a monologue, and Richard Fenchurch is now visited by other characters, both living and dead, who step out of his heated imagination and memory and onto the stage. Fenchurch tells his daughter Karen: "Ghosts. I see ghosts here, Karen, every night" (184). Yet the sane world of his family, the world from which Fenchurch has fled, is the very world that produced the stress that led to his present condition. Paradoxically Richard must remain in his madness to protect himself against the very conditions that have produced his madness.[47] All Richard has left is his madness, expressed at the end through his "dancing" (218-19), which enables him to endure the encroaching "blackness" of his situation (193).

Moreover, Stages is also the most direct and honest exploration of incest in Storey's world. Unlike The Restoration of Arnold Middleton the incestuous act in Stages does not occur quietly between the acts. Nor is it covered beneath the surface of an adolescent's sexual fantasies as in his novel A Prodigal Child. Incest is at the very center of this play and is the principal experience that has driven Fenchurch into his world of madness

Fenchurch has pursued the central affair of his life with his mother-in-law, Isabella, and identifies her death as the cause of his present madness: "The day she died I went quite mad" (205). In an interesting parallel, Bea, Isabella's daughter and Fenchurch's wife, leaves him and marries a younger man when she is fifty-one years old

(189). This is precisely the same age Isabella, Bea's mother, was when she fell in love with Richard: "I [Richard] was nineteen. She [Isabella] was fifty-one" (202). However, despite the symmetry in chronology, the crucial difference in the two relationships is that Bea is openly married to the Parliamentary Private Secretary to the Minister of Health (185). Bea's relationship is public and she accepts fully what she has done (189), whereas Richard has maintained a clandestine incestuous affair with his mother-in-law in which he was frequently mistaken for her son (204).

Somewhat incredibly, moreover, we are expected to believe that the affair that began when Richard was "nineteen" (202) and lasted until Isabella's death at "seventy-nine" (205) was only disclosed to one other person, Richard's psychiatrist, Marion.   Neither his wife nor his daughters—nor anyone else, for that matter—has ever had any knowledge of this affair. Richard assures Marion: "We were never discovered" (203).

Unfortunately, Stages reads much better than it plays[48] and is, of all Storey's dramas, with the possible exception of "Caring" (1992), a one-act, experimental companion piece to Stages, the least accessible and the least dramatic of his plays. Although it is courageous in exploring the implications of an illicit and "incestuous" affair between Fenchurch and his mother-in-law, a lovely woman, half Lebanese and half Celt, with dark skin and red hair (202), it unfortunately does so without evoking any feeling or particular insight into the nature of such an extended and complex relationship. The two remained committed, as it were, for the remainder of Isabella's life, and their very last tryst occurred when she was "seventy-nine" and Richard was "forty-seven" (205), a secret and protracted relationship of twenty-eight years.

However, as in Life Class, a play to be discussed later, Storey employs language rather than drama to explicate the affair and the subsequent bouts of madness that pursued and even hospitalized Richard (186) after the death of Isabella. We are told repeatedly what has happened and how to interpret what has happened, and predictably this evokes neither feeling nor understanding—indeed, not even compassion, so excessively pathetic is Richard on occasion at not being fully accepted as the intelligent artist he believes himself to be.[49] Perhaps it will remain as Storey's principal closet drama, for it is beautifully and poetically written.[50] Moreover, it does offer a picture of madness as the final option that has been taken to ensure survival, if indeed *survival* is the correct word, as Fenchurch slips deeper and deeper into the "blacknesses" that have been afflicting him (193). At the end, Fenchurch is left "dancing" by himself—a striking dramatic metaphor in contrast to the endless static chatter that preceded it—in the imagined presence of Rebecca, his next door neighbor, confidante and sometimes lover (210–11), who has been evoked by Richard to keep him "company" in the final, frenetic aria of the play.

Here the playwright enters directly into Richard's madness, allowing him to dance, perhaps in the desperate but futile hope of warding off the terrors of his loneliness and the painful memories that are now gathering force and relentlessly closing in upon him. He dances "for the dead," for his father and Isabella, and he dances for his "family" whom he believes he "sold" in a "covenant" to become an artist (219). His dancing figure now directly represents his madness—it is, in Laingian terms, "expressive of his existence" (*The Divided Self* 31), and the play ends with an image of Richard frozen in his frenetic desire to survive. It is a powerful dramatic image where Storey fuses the wild energy of Richard's madness into his behavior, and he leaves it for us, the audience, as the final image of his play: *"His dancing figure: moving.   Freezes. Light fades ."* (219)

The play begins with Richard reciting an ode, "Bella,"[51] to his mother-in-law that does not appear in the printed text of the play but is provided in the program. The poem introduces the theme of an incestuous love that is crucial to understanding the dramatic irony in the initial confrontation between Fenchurch and his daughter Karen— an irony that is maintained throughout the play:

Such love! Such was our care
beyond our incest to define
what love in love alone could find.[52]

The actual situation of the play is familiar Storey territory: children visiting their parents as the latter suffer in their declining years and isolation.[53] In this case, Richard, now divorced, is alone, but his ex-wife has learned from his next-door neighbor Rebecca that he is in serious trouble. He has been seen in town "pacing up and down" and when "spoken to" replies that he is "lost" (192). Karen then unsuccessfully tries to encourage her father to return to her home in Ardsley in Yorkshire, and he adamantly refuses to do so.

In the exchange between daughter and father, the poem that Richard reads at the beginning of the drama is made relevant. Both father and daughter discuss the first time Richard went home with Bea, whom he later married. Karen reminds her father that at this moment he fell in love, but the exchange is rich in dramatic irony, for we now know, as a result of the poem, that he indeed did fall in love at that critical moment in his life, but not with his bride-to-be but with her mother:

KAREN. You fell in love.
FENCHURCH. With her?

KAREN. With Mum.
FENCHURCH. Yes.
(Rises .)
I fell in love. (185-86)

For a moment, in this exchange, Fenchurch thinks his daughter may have in fact been aware of the truth of his illicit relationship—"With her?"—but Karen quickly becomes explicit, thereby establishing her ignorance. She thinks he is talking about her mother while we of course know he is talking about his mother-in-law.

Then Bea herself enters. She has presumably accompanied her daughter, although her presence lurking outside was never mentioned earlier by Karen. She too attempts to get Richard to return to Yorkshire. Interestingly, these two are the only characters who actually appear before Richard, for their entrance is choreographed in the play. When Karen comes, she first rings the doorbell and then enters by herself, having received the keys from the woman next door since Richard does not want any visitors at the moment (179). Similarly, when Bea enters, she too rings, and this is heard by both Karen and Richard (188), and Karen admits her mother into the room.

However, the appearance of the two remaining characters, Marion, the psychiatrist (200), and Rebecca, the next-door neighbor (208), is accomplished solely by a refocusing of the lights. In other words, they suddenly appear before Richard, although there is certainly no reason for Marion to be there—neither Karen nor Bea mention her—and Rebecca, who does lives next door, also appears quite unexpectedly, and from the nature of her dialogue (219), it appears that she too, while on the stage, is, like Marion, a projection of Richard's imagination.

There are also, as previously mentioned, "ghosts" who visit and revisit Richard, although they, like Marion and

Rebecca, do not appear on stage. He speaks of the visits of his dead father, who appears in various stages in his life. For example, his father appears when he is "old" and when he "died"; subsequently, he appears as a "child: a snotty nose," and then, most remarkably, Fenchurch is visited by his father in his parent's "cradle" on "the first Christmas of the century" when his father was born (201).[54]

Furthermore, Fenchurch's relationship with his father also sheds considerable light on the genesis of his madness. Fenchurch tells his daughter Karen that after he left school and married her mother the "melancholia" that he had been "prone to as a youth returned":

The darkness thickened. How do you reconcile writing novels and painting pictures to working down a mine? How do you reconcile my father's silicosis to the schooling I'd rejected? My life to his? His death to mine? (188)

There has always been the sharp guilt of his father's situation cutting deeply into Richard's psychological well-being. His father's suffering as a miner transformed itself into a mode of sacrifice that in Richard's judgment he has repaid with deep ingratitude. Instead of obtaining an education that would have provided him with a profession, Richard has become an artist, and this fact now forces him to compare the advantages he dismissed with the hard and unremitting life of his father who dug coal so that Richard would never have to go down into the pits.[55] Moreover, the very image of the artist, the one "painting pictures," rankles in his conscience as it is contrasted to his father's "working" in a mine. His life has become a complex symbol of treachery to his father's toil on his behalf.

Of course, being an artist is not working class, but it is an activity that his father, hardened by the puritanical circumstances of his life,[56] cannot and will not appreciate. In addition, the relationship between father and son takes on considerably more complexity when Richard informs us that the darkness in his father's life was not simply the result of coal dust. For like his son, Richard's father had serious mental difficulties that troubled him his entire life. Richard tells his wife:

My father, just before he died, hearing I'd been at the NLR [North London Royal, a mental hospital], told me he'd been afflicted by blacknesses himself. 'Well, you would,' I said, 'with all that bloody coal.' '*Mental* blacknesses,' he said. (193)

There is the suggestion here of a possible inheritance of the mental difficulties. His father sees in his son the same "blacknesses" that pursued him his entire life, but this connection is not pursued.   Father and son are both victims of intolerable conditions.   The difference, however, is that Richard succumbs while his father had endured the pressures of his life. He tells Richard: 'I've been up to here in blackness all my life,' holding his hand above his head (193).

Richard is also visited by his mother-in-law and lover, the dead Isabella (211), with whom he discusses his present relationship with Rebecca. This is rather novel dramaturgy. Rebecca, who is a projection of Richard, is on stage, but both characters, the flesh and blood Richard and the projection Rebecca, are visited by a ghost whom neither can see. Storey comes very close here to depicting the strange dramatic complexity of madness, and he perhaps would have succeeded had Rebecca and Isabella achieved any compelling presence in their own right. They are unfortunately phantoms, too thin to matter, and are lost in Fenchurch's long, singsong monologue about his relationship with Rebecca (211).

One other relationship in Richard's complexly troubled life is worth mentioning because it is there to intensify the horror of his loneliness and possibly to point a way to a rather tragic solution. After his divorce, he had a brief affair with an actress, Vivien, who auditioned for a film version of one of his novels (206). She, a heavy drinker, lived with him for a year and apparently was in as much psychological difficulty as Richard himself. He soon realized that Vivien, "since her husband left . . . had been looking for a place to die" (207). Finally, Vi kills herself and is found by Richard in the shed in his yard: "Beside her lay a bottle of household bleach" (207). This suicide is perhaps meant to point to the ultimate fate of Richard himself.

After Isabella's death, all Richard wants now is a place to die. His dancing at the end is perhaps a metaphor of this search—he is dancing to release himself, to die and to close out the darkness of his life. He will not return to his daughter's house in Yorkshire, and he has rejected psychiatry. In one of the few humorous exchanges in this rather dark play, Richard tells his wife what he thinks of his psychiatrist, Marion:

FENCHURCH. She'd have treated Christ with anti-depressants. She'd have given him Atavan for his night on the Mount of Olives. (189)

Stages demands comparison with *The Restoration of Arnold Middleton* (1967), Storey's first produced play. *The Restoration of Arnold Middleton* was criticized for not fully exploring the effects of the incestuous relationship between Arnold and his mother-in-law, but it at least achieved dramatic power and portrayed a breakdown on the stage. *Stages*, on the other hand, while exceedingly honest in probing a complex "incestuous" relationship,[57]

produces no corresponding effect of feeling and no particular understanding of Richard and Isabella's relationship
other than their initial physical attraction. It is a play that
reads like a long poem—lyrical, but cold, aloof, and
terribly unaffecting. Although it offers explanations for
Richard's breakdown—the guilt over his father and the
prolonged incestuous relationship—these events are
never explored dramatically. As a play, *Stages* must be
considered one of Storey's interesting failures. It does
present madness on the stage, but fails to provide us with
the insight and feeling to fully understand that condition.

Nevertheless, Storey's dramatic presentation of madness is quite impressive in its range and rich variety. We
have seen the voyage from sanity to madness in *The
Restoration of Arnold Middleton* even though the play
ends with a rather feeble and unconvincing attempt at
mental rehabilitation. We have further seen a complex
society in *Home*, where the playwright is able to incorporate a wide range of mad behavior as well as elevate his
play to considerable allegorical heights, suggesting, at the
play's conclusion, that the world is indeed threatened, not
by the mad, but by the sane. Moreover, in *Sisters* the deception of Adrienne can initially project the sole image of
sanity and innocence in what first appears as a completely
mad environment. Slowly Adrienne is unmasked as the
reality surrounding her is equally exposed. Indeed, the
worlds, both in *Home* and *Sisters*, suggest the deceptive
qualities of madness itself: those on the inside of a mental
institution—or those who have fled, for that matter—do
not appear any less sane than those on the outside.[58] In
fact, if anything, they initially appear sane, and, as in the
case of Adrienne, saner than those around her. At any
rate, as the plays demonstrate, the actions of the sane
characters, as R. D. Laing has argued, are often more dangerous, as well as treacherous to themselves and to others,

than the actions of those whom society has for its particular political reasons deemed "mad" (*The Divided Self* 27). And finally in *Stages* Storey probes madness itself as a mechanism of survival. At the end of the play, all Richard can do is begin "dancing" with the phantoms that appear before him on stage. His painful guilt over his father's life and death, his failed marriage, and his extended incestuous relationship have all forced him into a "blackness"; and that condition, in a strict Laingian application, is an expression of the intolerable conditions of his life. Richard is expressing his "existence as he experiences it" (*The Divided Self* 31), and that expression is his insanity. It is also his sole mode of survival.

NOTES

1. In two recent plays, *Early Days (1980)*, a Pinteresque drama of considerable power, and *The March on Russia* (1988), a family play structurally similar to Storey's early work like *In Celebration* (1969), the playwright probes the near madness of elderly characters.   In Storey's world, even if his characters can successfully avoid madness in their youth, when they are most vulnerable, given the intense pressures placed upon the young to adjust, the possibility for a breakdown persists—there is evidently no protection in one's final years.

2. Storey informs us that the original title of the play was *To Die With The Philistines* (Findlater 25).

3. Storey misses the opportunity to work here with the potentially mystifying as well as humorous dramatic situation of blood relatives—or putative blood relatives, as in the case of *Sisters*—not being able to recognize each other, a situation similar to the initial confrontation between Dodge and his grandson Vince in Sam Shepard's *Buried Child* (1978). Of course there is a significant difference: in Shepard's play, Vince is Dodge's grandson; in Storey's *Sisters*, Mrs. Donaldson simply assumes the role of mother. Nevertheless, Shepard perpetuates the confusion with considerable dramatic effect and thematic significance of the family's confusing and tangled bonds of kinship, while Storey almost immediately clears up the bewilderment and does so quite

unnecessarily (*Sisters* 62), since the effects of the family relationships in the play would have considerably more meaning as well as dramatic impact if we were to discover the reality of these affiliations without being so explicitly informed.

4. Fenchurch is the name of a minor character, referred to as "Fenny," in the *Changing Room*. This, yet again, displays Storey's penchant for using identical names in different works, although in this case there is no similarity between the two men—the footballer is described as a "neatly groomed man . . . self-contained, perhaps even at times a vicious man" (96) and the artist Richard Fenchurch of *Stages* is a complex and deeply disturbed man. However, Corrigan is the same last name of the older woman whose affair with the young Bryan is central to the novel *A Prodigal Child*. Thus, Mrs. Fay Corrigan of the novel returns here as Fenchurch's mother-in-law and lover, Mrs. Isabella Corrigan--indeed, in the play she is, although dead, central to his life: "I live—and still live—for her alone" (204).

5. *Stages* (1992) probes the sexual relationship that should have been probed in *The Restoration of Arnold Middleton* between Arnold and Edie—a relationship that led to Arnold's subsequent breakdown.

6. Laura Weaver informs us that in "Bernard Bergonzi's 1968 interview," the playwright Storey recognized the affinity between himself and R. D. Laing, although he claimed that he came to the same conclusions through intuition, whereas the psychiatrist employed "intellectual methods" (Hutchings, *Casebook* 124).

7. For a critique of Laing, see Lillian Feder, who accuses him, in his "rigid division of mental and social experience," of developing a "mystical construct" that is sharply refuted by the literature of madness itself. Madness "more often portrays despair, chaos, pain, and emptiness than it does transcendental oneness" (*Madness in Literature*, 280–83). Furthermore, current scientific research completely disputes Laing's explanantion of schizophrenia as a political event. For a thoroguh discussion of such evidence, see E. Fuller Torrey, et al., *Schizophrenia and Manic-Depressive Disorder: The Biological Roots of Mental Illness as Revealed by the Landmark Study of Identical Twins* (New York: Basic Books, 1994). This six-year study of identical twins where one is schizophrenic and the other is normal documents the organic and neurological basis for mental illness as well as the importance of genetic factors in the disease's etiology.

8. Storey originally intended to have Arnold commit suicide at the play's conclusion. In fact, Storey still has serious misgivings about the revisions of his first produced drama, revisions that suggest somewhat feebly an accommodation between Arnold and the world around him (*The Restoration of Middleton* 70). Storey feels that he failed in the revision to follow out the "logic" of the story, the logic evidently leading, directly and inexorably, to Arnold's destruction through suicide (Hutchings, *The Plays* 10). Lindsay Anderson, Storey's director and principal collaborator, assures us that Storey still believes that his drama "wasn't fully achieved . . ."(Hutchings, *Casebook* 4). Interestingly, William Gaskill, another British director who worked at the Royal Court and is primarily associated with the playwright Edward Bond, believes that Storey, whom he genuinely admires, never in his subsequent work equaled "the raw passion" of *The Restoration of Arnold Middleton* (109–110).

9. Storey's novel *Pasmore* (1972) returns to the theme of the potentially lethal effects of sexual repression. It alone, in its conclusion, appears to have worked out a mode of survival for characters so torturously repressed as Colin Pasmore; and Hutchings is quite wrong in concluding that the "personal reintegration" worked out by Pasmore is similar to Arnold Middleton's (*The Plays*, 57). Arnold has been destroyed; Pasmore saves himself.

10. In *Flight into Camden*—a novel in the first-person and Storey's only work of fiction where a woman is the central character—Margaret, the heroine, is so oppressed by the restrictive circumstances of her life that she finally escapes from her home and runs off to Camden Town in London to live with her lover, Howarth, an older married man. Her action devastates her family living in a small town in Yorkshire, and they are committed to forcing her to return. Her father, a miner, has stopped working, so distressed is he over his daughter's behavior (199). Here in London, however, in some of Storey's most explicitly sensual prose, Margaret discovers her own freedom and her own sexuality as an independent woman. This liberation, unfortunately, is short lived, for Margaret is subsequently maneuvered into returning home by her brother Michael, who claims falsely that their mother is seriously ill (198); and home to Margaret is a "prison" (202). Unfortunately, while Margaret is away, Howarth departs from their London flat, as he backs out of the relationship through his own weakness. The novel ends with Margaret utterly devastated by the betrayal

and left in a psychologically crippled condition—clearly a form of incipient madness brought on by both the treachery of her lover and her forced return to a world that is utterly unacceptable, but a world from which she is unable to escape. Her liberation in London has not gone far enough to ensure her future independence. Margaret, like Arnold Middleton, now appears imprisoned in her own solitude. Storey describes her as almost disembodied in the final pages as she awakens to voices in the garden of her brother's home (219). The voices at the end have an eerie tone, suggesting a considerable psychological distance between Margaret and those around her. She has apparently crossed over the line, severing herself from her family bonds and the repressive community of which they are a part. She will very likely slip deeper into herself, unable to live within her "prison" and equally unable to escape from it. In a Laingian analysis, Margaret's behavior is clearly inappropriate, but she is not sick. Her withdrawal into herself is an effort to cope with the intolerable conditions of her situation or, as Laing would say, Margaret's "behavior is a function of experience" and, presumably, if her experience was changed Margaret's inappropriate behavior would change (*The Politics of Experience* 25).

11. In many respects, *The Restoration of Arnold Middleton* is very much a drama within the dark comedic tradition as defined by J. L. Styan: "Dark comedy may initially anatomize, but it does it to free us of stereotyped but arbitrary attitudes. . . . The farcical and the pathetic will flow by imperceptible motions into one another, as they do when life is seen at a distance, as when age reflects on youth; or they will be violently thrown together, as when we stand close at the centre of it" (277—278).

12. Perhaps Nell in Beckett's *Endgame* most succinctly expresses the essence of tragicomedy: "Nothing is funnier than unhappiness. . . .. (18).

13. The erotic obsession with older women is, as previously noted, a frequent occurrence in Storey's work. In this regard, Susan Mauk Clark, in an unpublished doctoral dissertation, comments on the puzzling circumstances of young Machen's involvement in *This Sporting Life*: "For a man [Machen] 'at the top of the heap' to be engrossed by an unattractive widow with two children is difficult to fathom unless one understands Storey's obsession with physical and spiritual disharmony. Even then, some questions remain unanswerable" (19). Actually, Machen, like Arnold Middleton, despite their differences in sensibili-

ties, intelligence, and education, are both victims of a puritanical code of sexual conduct, a mode of behavior which identifies the older woman, particularly a widow with children, like Mrs. Hammond, and presumably Arnold's mother-in-law, Mrs. Edie Ellis, since she is also a widow (*The Resotration of Arnold Middleton* 3), as sexually available and easily disposable.   For a good discussion of the sexual morality practiced among the miners and their girlfriends and wives, see Denis, Heriques, and Slaughter's ethnological study *Coal Is Our Life*   in which the behavior of the men and women of Ashton, a coal mining town in Yorkshire, is closely examined (210–33). Unfortunately, the study does not detail the obsessional interest in older women, but it does describe the terrible gulf that exists between the sexes and helps explain the painfully perplexing behavior that occurs between men and women—behavior that is frequent in Storey's dramas.

14. Arnold's witty as well as morbid conclusion to the stanza points to the possible mode of suicide that he may be contemplating at this early moment in the play. This will be discussed later when the function of the sword—the sole piece of memorabilia that Arnold retains of his entire collection (67)—is examined in terms of the play's end.

15. Although Arnold claims that Sheila has asked him out (36) for the evening, it is very possible that he has told the young student about the evening's party and this would explain her being in front of the Middleton home on the night of the party and her subsequently being invited in by Hanson who arrives with Maureen (35), an extremely clever element of dramaturgy on Storey's part.

16. Lindsay Anderson informs us that the play was originally written for television, but was rejected by the networks because of Arnold's seduction of his mother-in-law (Hutchings, *Casebook* 3–4).

17. Arnold, despite considerable differences, resembles Blakely in the novel *Radcliffe*   (1963). Blakely, who is older than Arnold, is a minor character in the novel, but like Arnold he is terribly sexually repressed and is a man who is very alone, his pain covered to some extent by his flamboyance and eccentricity—characteristics that can also be applied to Arnold. Finally, however, Blakely cracks and commits suicide by slitting his own throat after he has murdered his entire family. Blakely is destroyed because he can neither cope with his powerful sexual repression nor possess the object of his love, Victor Tolson. Furthermore, prior to these crimes, he, like Arnold (67), delivered an

"extremely articulate appeal for the strengthening and preservation of the monarchy. . ."(351). Such a paean is perhaps, in a Storey work, an indication that the character making the plea is cracking up. Moreover, Blakely's self-destruction parallels what probably was intended as the final fate for Arnold Middleton if Storey had, as he himself has admitted, remained faithful to the "logic" of his play (Hutchings, *The Plays* 10). This would at least explain the presence of the sword in Arnold's hand at the end of the drama. Perhaps it was originally intended that with this weapon Arnold, like Blakely, would slit his own throat.

18. In a sharply contrasting point of view, William Hutchings sees Arnold's paean to kingship as indicative of a "symbolic incarnation of the transcendent qualities that modern life lacks" (*The Plays* 48), and further identifies the presence of the sword as "a symbol of permanence that surpasses the flux of history. . . . Rifles rust, erode, and fall apart. . . . But swords, while rusting too, preserve down to their last grain an emblem of truth. Instruments of honour ..." (51), a most questionable observation in both respects. Hutchings further concludes that Arnold is indeed restored through a "personal reintegration," although he never explains how this is precisely accomplished, and why the play, despite its "seriousness," is simply a "deft and witty comedy" (57).

19. This act together with its powerfully destructive manifestations is central to *Stages* (1992), Storey's most recent drama.

20. Presumably Storey would concur since he supports Laing's conception of madness as a political label and not as a medical condition (Hutchings, *Casebook* 124).

21. Arnold's incompatibility with his wife is not simply sexual, although this is clearly the most important element in their relationship. He is also one who lives happily amidst the clutter of his possessions while his wife is obsessively committed to domestic tidiness.

22. I am using the term "realism" here in the sense defined by Ruby Cohn: "I understand realism as the mimetic representation of contemporary middle-class reality. . . . The heir of the well-made play, it too is well made in linking cause and effect within a plot. The characters behave with sociological and psychological credibility; members of the broadening middle class, they display the effects of its education and conventions . . ." (2).

23. Ruby Cohn also identifies resemblances to Chekhov's influence in *Home* 's "penchant for interstitial meanings" (*Retreats* 36).

24. In a rather witty, but not terribly serious interview of both David Storey and his director Lindsay Anderson, Guy Flatley learns from the playwright himself that prior to the New York City production of *Home* he had never seen "a Pinter Play"; clearly we, as well as Guy Flatley, must doubt the seriousness of Storey's remarks ("I Never Saw a Pinter Play" 1, 5).

25. Harry tells Jack as well as Kathleen and Marjorie about his brief previous experience as an actor: "Well, as a matter of fact ... not your Hamlets, of course, your Ophelias; more the little bystander..." (57). Harry's admission strikes a note of comic parody and sounds curiously like T. S. Eliot's Prufrock who similarly comments that he is not "Prince Hamlet" but an "attendant lord. .." ("The Love Song of J. Alfred Prufrock," *The Complete Poems* 7). Harry, like Prufrock, sees his life as distinctly non–heroic and subservient.

26. Indeed, in Pinter's case, considering that both Gus and Ben are hired killers, their sentimental and incredulous reaction to the old man's accident is a superb example of humor at its very darkest.

27. Although considerably more coarse and more fully drawn as full characters, Kathleen and Marjorie are similar to Pinter's two old women in his witty Revue Sketch of lower-class women "The Black and White" (*Complete Works: Two* 240–43).

28. Ruby Cohn considers Storey's use of the name "Alfred" suggestive of "the name of Britain's great king of the Anglo-Saxon Chronicles" (*Retreats* 40). The play does reverberate with names in English history—"Darwin," "Newton," "Milton," "Sir Walter Raleigh . . . who lost his head"(79)—suggesting that the former great British Empire that gave birth to and nurtured figures of immense historical importance has now turned in on itself, becoming in the process a lunatic asylum. A specifically political interpretation of the play is offered by Richard Dutton who sees the influence of "Renaissance tragicomedy," particularly *The Tempest*, on the structure of *Home*. Dutton argues that *Home* is in effect a social allegory on postimperial Great Britain where the empire's sun has set; the microcosmic world as represented in the disillusion and purposelessness of Harry's and Jack's dialogue directly reflects upon the macrocosmic society, modern England (*Modern Tragicomedy and the British Tradition* 159-160).

29. Beckett's influence is also evident in stage activities, particularly in Jack's card tricks (81), which are reminiscent of the vaudevillian antics of Vladimir and Estragon in *Waiting for Godot* (1954).

30. Compare this setting to the rather elaborate and specific stage requirements—requirements typical, incidentally, of well-made, realistic plays—specified in *The Restoration of Arnold Middleton* (1) and *In Celebration* (9) and one can see how Storey's view of stage space is evolving into a simpler and bleaker dramatic territory, a territory that can support the desolate vision necessary for *Home*. In this regard, the critic Richard Dutton has emphasized the material emptiness of the modern tragicomic landscape: "tragicomedy seems not at all concerned with prosperity, conspicuous consumption or designer performance. It is by comparison, a 'poor theatre' with minimal props and little surplus. . . . its outcast characters resemble at times latter-day consumers stripped of their adornments and their illusions, literally unrecognizable, forced to act out their parts with no good reason for doing so" (*Tragicomedy and Contemporary Culture* 7).

31. Storey informs us that the metal worktable "and the table alone" left at the conclusion of *The Contractor* (1970) provided the dramatic impulse that blossomed into *Home* (Findlater 113).

32. This of course contrasts sharply with the suspense evoked in *The Restoration of Arnold Middleton* which, as we have seen, precisely addresses the question of what will happen next.

33. Alfred's lobotomy represents a good example of how the sane, according to Laing, are "dangerous . . . to others" (*The Divided Self* 27). Regardless of Alfred's bizarre behavior, nothing he has done can ever compensate him for the cruel surgical procedure he has undergone at the behest of "sane" authority.

34. These lines parody Gaunt's paean to England in Shakespeare's *King Richard II* (II.i. 44–72):

This royal throne of kings, this scept'red isle,
This earth of majesty, this seat of Mars,
This other Eden, demiparadise,
This fortress built by Nature for herself
Against infection and the hand of war,
. . . This England. . . .

35. *Sisters* is a play for which Storey is not certain of its specific date of composition and tells us that it may have been written "at some time between 1974 and 1978" (Hutchings, *The Plays* 11).

36. *Sisters* is only one of two works of Storey's where women are central in the narrative. The other work is the novel *Flight into Camden* (1960) where Margaret tells her story in the first-person.

37. Adrienne hear sounds very much like Margaret in *Flight into Camden* (1960) who similarly flees from the puritanical restrictive home of her birth.

38. Perhaps it was intended on Carol's part that her sister would never learn the truth of the home serving as a brothel. She simply was not certain how long Adrienne would stay and perhaps thought—the play is not clear on this point—that she could successfully deceive her sister not only about the home but about her role as a prostitute as well.

39. *Sisters* is very much a work in the contemporary naturalistic tradition as defined by Ruby Cohn. Naturalistic drama follows the same sociological and psychological principles that inform realism, but the characters are working class and this limits the scope of their behavior (*Retreats from Realism* 4).

40. Hutchings (*Plays* 136–37) points out the parallels in *Sisters* to both Tennessee Williams's *A Street Car Named Desire* (1947) and Harold Pinter's *The Homecoming* (1965). Needless to say, *Sisters* suffers unfavorably in comparison to both of these major contemporary dramatic works, but it is still a play of considerable merit.

41. A creation of similar comic power, perhaps the only other character in the entire Story canon to equal Crawford, is the preposterous R. N. Wilcox in the novel *A Temporary Life* (1973).

42. Laing would argue that Adrienne is experiencing herself as the agent of a "Second Coming" (102), as possible mother of the Savior. We are required, therefore, "to orientate ourselves" to understand her "mode of being-in-the world" and we must "relate" her actions to her experience (*The Divided Self* 32). In other words, as far as Laing is concerned—and, for that matter, David Storey—Adrienne is "expressing in radical terms the stark truth" of her experience. And it is precisely her experience of her "existence" that is her "insanity" (*The Divided Self* 38).

43. For example, the early exchanges between Mrs. Donaldson and Adrienne over their relationship to Carol seems to be the work of an inexperienced dramatist desiring to make certain that the audience

absolutely understands what is occurring (59-62). The relationship of Mrs. Donaldson and Carol are clearly understood in the subtext of the exchange and do not require such explicit exposition.

44. Since *Sisters* has many structural similarities to *A Streetcar Named Desire* it is possible that Blanche's trunk, which is very central in scene 10 of William's drama (151–62), influenced Storey to incorporate a trunk in his play.

45. Interestingly, and somewhat amusingly, even Tom's first marriage, when he was eighteen, is with an older woman, a relationship which ended disastrously. Storey's male characters frequently appear obsessed with older women with whom they have relationships with unfortunate consequences.

46. In its investigation into memory in order to understand the present moment, it is similar conceptually to Beckett's *Krapp's Last Tape*; however, Krapp's monologue, in contrast to Fenchurch's, is intensely dramatic. Both reflect upon lost loves, although Krapp actually, through the device of the tape recorder, talks to himself as a younger man—the old Krapp responding to the younger Krapp; and both plays end in a terrible solitude: Richard dancing frantically by himself to ward off the approaching terror of his madness (219) and as "the tape runs on in silence" Krapp comments to himself: "Here I end this reel. Box—(pause)—three, spool. . . . Perhaps my best years are gone. But I wouldn't want them back. . . . No, I wouldn't want them back" (28).

47. Laing would undoubtedly concur with this diagnosis. Although Richard is schizophrenic and clearly behaving in an unacceptable manner, he is nonetheless reacting honestly to the stress of his life. He is, like Adrienne in *Sisters*, "expressing . . . the stark truth of his situation," which is his "insanity" (*The Divided Self* 38).

48. Frank Rich's comments on *Stages*, although quite severe, are characteristic of the play's reception: "Alan Bates . . . does his best to mime the poetic riffs and turgid emotions of an almost perversely undramatic exercise" (C9).

49. For example, Fenchurch informs us that even though he is the son of a coal miner he "passed the eleven-plus at the age of nine: an exam intended to be taken by every child at the age of eleven" (187).

50. Consider, for example, the lines that describe the initial moment of seduction between Richard and his mother-in-law. In this quote, I have retained the typography to indicate the poetic structure

employed:

The path she took me to at the back of the house was encroached by shrubs on one side, on the other by a dell. I took her hand. When I glanced back I saw her face, dark, her red hair couched against the collar of her coat—a loose-fitting garment, drawn in at the waist—dark green—and trimmed at the cuffs and collar by dark brown fur. Her hand was delicate and thin. I was conscious of the coolness of its palm, 'The hand,' I thought, 'of another man's wife, pregnant with the intimacy of their twenty-odd year marriage.'

I was nineteen. She was fifty-one.

We reached a bank, With a final scramble I went in front, stooped, took both her hands, and drew her to me.

How long we stood there I've no idea. (202)

51. "Bella" is not included in Storey's recently published book of his collected poetry, *Storey's Lives* (1992); the poem was obviously written for the production of *Stages*.

52. Program, Royal National Theatre Production, *Stages*, 1992.

53. For example, in *The March on Russia* (1988), the play immediately preceding *Stages*, the children learn that their father, Tommy Pasmore, has been engaging in petty acts of thievery in the small seaside town where he has retired.

54. The situation of mad people experiencing their as younger than they are also occurs in *Home* when Marjorie observes that Alfred thinks that he is "older than his dad" (70).

55. The guilt experienced by the artistic and professional children of the working class is a principal theme in Storey's family plays, like *In Celebration* (1969) and *The March on Russia* (1988), which will be discussed later in detail.

56. See Stinson for a discussion of the miners' hostility to artistic or intellectual work (131–43).

57. There is of course a very significant difference in the two relationships: Arnold simply seduces Edie in a single act of lust; Richard and Isabella, as we have seen, maintained their relationship for twenty-eight years until Isabella died at seventy-nine (205).

58. As Kalson noted, the line separating sanity from madness in Storey's universe is elusive (111).

3

PLAYS OF WORK

Between 1970 and 1974, David Storey wrote three plays
that focus upon men and women at work: *The Contractor*
(1970), *The Changing Room* (1971), and *Life Class* (1974).
Each of these plays makes a work process their central
event. An unfolding, dynamic image is examined as it is
constructed or performed, each element of the procedure
carefully documented: the erection and disassembly of a
marquee for a wedding ceremony[1]; the activities of a professional rugby team before, during, and after a match; and
the instruction of art students in drawing the nude model
in a life class. In the first two plays, there is no principal
character and there is no discernible plot, except, as noted,
for the completion of the task at hand. The marriage ceremony, for which the tent is erected, occurs offstage during the play's intermission, and the rugby game, for which
the players have assembled and engaged in pre-play
preparation, occurs offstage as well.[2] In both these dramas, moreover, there is no single dramatic event of central and unifying significance: the activities are begun,

worked upon steadily, and completed. There are not even any surprises—what we expect to happen is all that happens. Nevertheless, out of the multitude of seemingly trivial events—men slowly and methodically setting up a tent or rugby players dressing and warming up for a match—Storey develops dramatic structures that have been identified variously as "poetic naturalism" (Cave 139) or "documentary realism" (Hayman 58).

It is only later, however, when we reflect upon the literal situations on the stage that dark and complex considerations occur. Ruby Cohn has noted that "David Storey's plays conceal their national resonance so adroitly that an audience has to absorb it as if by osmosis." Ruby Cohn quotes Storey on his structural intention: "The purely literal level has to work first. And perhaps work only at that level. Leave the audience to fathom the symbolic level" (*Retreats* 35).

Life Class, like *The Contractor* and *The Changing Room*, is also a drama about work. In this play, the work endeavor is artistic and intellectual—the training of art students to draw from the nude model. However, unlike the two previous plays, there is in *Life Class* a principal character, Allott, the art instructor. There is also a carefully moderated plot as well as a principal event—the simulated rape of the nude model by two students before the assembled class, including Allott himself (224–26). More importantly, the dramatic purpose in *Life Class* is significantly different from Storey's intention in his two previous plays. Now Storey incorporates the elements of his drama into an extended dramatic lecture upon the nature of the aesthetic event itself. The literal event—the simulated rape—is extensively interpreted to provide us with the essence of artistic expression. In effect, *Life Class* attempts to define what had been dramatized in *The Contractor* as well as *The Changing Room*. In *Life Class*,

Storey does not leave to the audience the freedom "to fathom the symbolic level" of his play as he suggested to Peter Ansorge (Cohn 35). Through Allott's mouth, Storey delivers his detailed analysis of the aesthetic event, and there is nothing left for the members of the audience to interpret. The play itself is a statement of interpretation as well as a general aesthetic to be applied, presumably, to all artistic expression.

The Contractor, produced in 1970, is Storey's first experiment with his new poetic, naturalistic style—the style of *cinéma vérité,* or documentary realism, as already mentioned. This form of theater, as one critic has observed, precludes

star parts and a conventional narrative plot in favour of theatrical teamwork to create a new version of the ancient notion of the theatre as microcosm. Stage business takes on the status of dramatic action and the dialogue is spare. . . . It approximates to "writing degree zero." [3] (Morgan 558)

Interestingly, a detail of this play, the white table, left on stage at the conclusion of the drama, led directly to *Home* (1971),[4] a play that was primarily discussed as a dramatic depiction of madness, but a play that also incorporates the complex naturalistic techniques introduced in *The Contractor.*

The *Contractor* employs a work process as a technical device that is central to the structural significance of the drama. This device, the erecting and disassembling of the wedding tent,[5] functions as the primary image that defines the wedding ceremony, which occurs offstage during the intermission as well as hinting at the possible fate of the marriage being celebrated; it also defines the various relationships among the characters in the play—the relationships among the members of Ewbank's family as well as the workers in his employ. Among a variety of possible

interpretations, *The Contractor* is a drama about impermanence, about inevitable, yet unpredictable change,
about commitments made only to be later broken, about
the intractable transience of all deeply complex human
experiences.[6] Benedict Nightingale, in a extended discussion of *The Contractor*, claims that the play, a "humane
and resonant" work, is intentionally "ambiguous" and
open ended and not subject to any particular interpretation (429), a critical view, incidentally, supported by Storey
himself:

> I get letters from people who ask me, does it mean this, does it mean
> that, and I often see some justice in their suggestions. And still the play
> is not confined to any one of these definitions; it contains the possibility
> of them, but it still continues to make sense—and complete sense—as
> the story of these men who put up the tent, and that's that. I think it's
> very important for me to leave all the options open. (qtd. in
> Nightingale 430)

On a very simple level, a tent is an ephemeral structure, and regardless of the care and devotion with which it
was put up, it is meant to be short lived. As it sits on the
stage, its vulnerability is evident. The knowledge that it
will be taken down is inherent in the image itself—it is after all a tent.[7] Yet it is the central controlling image, its
very transience, as we shall see, symbolizes the weak
bonds among the men who construct it as well as the frag-
ile union that the impending marriage is about to conse-
crate.

The Ewbank family gathers to celebrate a marriage, a
ritual intended to secure life-long commitments, yet the
drama's "essence," in the sense enunciated by Peter
Brook—its "silhouette," so to speak—quite ironically cele-
brates the ephemeral nature of human relationships.[8] We
watch the lovely and delicate tent go up (208), yet we also
see its subsequent abuse as a result of the ensuing festivi-

ties (217), and finally its disassembly as it is carted away unceremoniously (239). The image of this ongoing event—the tent going up and coming down—resonates powerfully, almost in a biblical sense,[9] in the memory of the viewers, certainly long after the individual stories of the characters—stories that echo and reinforce the theme of impermanence and marginality—are long forgotten.

Storey uses the tent as a device to imagistically encompass both human hope at the beginning of the work process, joy at its culmination, when the graceful tent provokes the Ewbank family to dance in response to its loveliness (214-215), and as a powerful note of sadness and loss when the tent is disassembled and carted off the stage at the play's conclusion. We begin with a stage with three bare tent poles and we end with a stage with three bare tent poles (151; 246). All this activity, all this energy, and what indeed has happened? What has been produced of lasting significance?[10] Moreover, this structural device, as Austin Quigley has noted, represents "an important aspect of Storey's originality as a dramatist—his ability to transform conventional technical devices into structural images which control the thematic implications of the plays" ("Emblematic Structure" 260).

As the tent is the central device, Ewbank, a man of immense personal appeal, despite his gruff and gauche behavior,[11] is the most important character, but he is by no means a conventional protagonist. This is clearly a play without a hero. Like the tent itself, Ewbank is pivotal to all the action that swirls frantically around the busy and cluttered stage, for it is he, as the tent contractor who sets the work into motion and as the father of the bride, who represents the blood connection to all the other characters, save one, who appear on stage. There is only Maurice, the prospective bridegroom, a medical doctor and a curiously flaccid character who weaves in and out of the action of the drama, sharply contrasting with the robust and rowdy workmen. Ewbank himself comments on the insubstantial, almost wraith-like demeanor of his future son-in-law to his foreman Kay: "She's [Claire] marrying a bloody aristocrat, Kay. He's so refined if it wasn't for his britches he'd be invisible" (176).

The accuracy of this comment seems to be borne out in Maurice's subsequent behavior. When we first meet him, he is the only one who is unhappy about the wedding being performed in the tent that is currently being erected (179), and rather lamely rejects joining in the efforts of putting up the tent, an activity in which even Paul, Ewbank's aimless and phlegmatic son, has become happily engaged. Maurice tells Paul, "If I didn't feel so exhausted I'd have given you a hand" (180). And when Fitzpatrick, the burly and boisterous Irishman and mate of Marshall on the work crew, directly asks Maurice and Claire how they are feeling before their wedding night, the bridegroom again responds in his typical dry and unresponsive manner:

FITZPATRICK. And what's it like, then, to be the happy couple? The blushing bride and the handsome groom?
MAURICE. All right, I suppose. (201)

Claire herself never even bothers to answer Fitzpatrick's friendly request, her silence suggesting a reaction that might be identified as insensitivity toward menial workers or excused as nervousness, given the distraction of her impending marriage; but the silence may in fact conceal deep anxiety concerning the marriage itself—a union that, consistent with the play's theme of impermanence, will not survive. As a result, she may be unable to answer Fitzpatrick, for fear of blurting out feelings that are better left unsaid.

When we do see Maurice and Claire together on stage, there is no indication of a strong emotional commitment between the two. In fact, there is no indication of any commitment, regardless of its intensity. At the very best, they seem to oddly amuse each other. Before their wedding day, in the newly erected tent, they do dance together as they are joined by other members of the Ewbank family, but their dancing alone appears mechanical and tentative, as well as joyless; and revealingly Claire suggests in an oblique sardonic comment that the marriage is occurring simply because events are falling into place under the weight of their own momentum—the guests have arrived, the tent has been set up, and the ceremony is imminent.

For example, Maurice thinks there ought to be "a few drinks" served [12] but is cautioned to wait for the marriage festivities by Mrs. Ewbank:

MRS. EWBANK. Oh, there's plenty of time for that.
CLAIRE. In any case. We're not hitched.
MAURICE. Not yet.
MRS. EWBANK. Oh, now. Don't let's start on that.
CLAIRE (*gestures at tent*). If only for this we have no option.
  (*They laugh.*) (214)

What is interesting here is that Claire has obviously been commenting on the possibility of not marrying and suggests in a rather phlegmatic manner—a manner consistent with both her and Maurice's behavior—that the wedding is proceeding simply because of the rush of impending circumstances. If the tent had not been erected, the marriage perhaps could have been avoided. In addition, her uncertainty has obviously been mentioned much more forcefully and frequently in the past, as evidenced by her mother's desire to quickly stifle all further skeptical comments concerning her forthcoming marriage. Finally Claire does laugh, but her laughter, like her previous silence in response to Fitzpatrick's question, appears as a cover for her distress rather than as a simple expression of pleasure.

Storey develops the future dark side of the marriage less explicitly but much more dramatically through the nature of the dancing itself on stage. While Paul and his mother dance with "*some pleasure*," Claire and Maurice only dance "tentatively" (214); and they finally break off their own dance to watch Ewbank dance with his wife "round the whole tent" (215). Although Ewbank's dancing is described as "firm and implacable," it is nevertheless authentically indicative of the man himself, or as Storey indicates it is dancing that is "entirely characteristic of himself" (215). But it is only the prospective bride and groom who dance briefly and without any feeling, an activity strongly suggesting the emotional coldness that is in store for them as a married couple.

Moreover, the relationship between Claire and Maurice has not gone completely unnoticed by the workmen. Marshall, one of the two Irishmen on the job, a Protestant who has himself been married three times (164), believes that Maurice and Claire are "both heading for trouble" (224). While it is true that Marshall bases his assumption on the general belief that marriage "as an institution . . . is all washed out" (224), his comments nevertheless cannot help but reinforce the rather dark reality that the drama suggests is the future for the young newlyweds.

Finally, and most interestingly, Claire and Maurice are never seen as a married couple, even though the marriage occurs in the interval between act 2 and act 3; indeed, their absence has to be noted, as they alone, among the twelve members of the cast, are the only ones who do not appear in act 3. Even more importantly, it is their marriage for which the wedding celebration has been arranged and the wedding marquee raised, and their absence, like the tent's final disappearance, serves pointedly to underscore the general theme in Storey's drama: the impermanence of all human relationships.

The workers themselves are examined as marginal inhabitants in society, those living on its very edge and completely dependent for their economic survival upon Ewbank's generosity, since no one else will employ them, so dubious are their work and personal backgrounds: the two rowdy and boisterous Irishmen, who have already been mentioned; the Englishman Bennet, who has himself suffered through marital difficulties with his wife's infidelities and, as a result, suffers as the cruel butt of the Irishmen's jokes, particularly Fitzpatrick's (225); the obviously hard-working and responsible foreman Kay, who is married and the father of three daughters, but who has also served time in prison for embezzlement (191); and the mildly retarded and ingenuous Glendenning, a typical Storey innocent, drawn with considerable compassion and insight, and without a trace of condescension[13]:

EWBANK: I employ anybody here . . . . Anybody who'll work. Miners who've coughed their lungs up, fitters who've lost their finger. . . . I take on all those that nobody else'll employ. (175)

The very marginality of the workmen themselves contributes to the general sense of transience associated with the erecting and disassembly of the tent and the rather tentative and unfeeling relationship between Claire and Maurice. For example, the strongest relationship among the workers is clearly between Fitzpatrick and Marshall, who are unfailingly united in their boisterous and often crude behavior. If events become difficult, as they occasionally do, they at least have each other and can depend on the strength of their friendship and each other's humor, as they always appear to laugh as if on cue. Yet when Fitzpatrick is fired—quite justifiably, given his aggressive bantering and sharp indifference to the suffering of the other men—he expects his friend Marshall to quit and sever himself from the work crew. He learns that their relationship, however strong it may have appeared in the past, is in effect quite easily fractured:

FITZPATRICK (To Marshall). Are you coming?
MARSHALL. Well, now ... If there's one of us to be out of work ... better that the other sticks to what he can. (230)

This does not moderate Fitzpatrick's feelings, and he responds to his mate in bitterness: "Aye. I suppose you're right" and then labels all present, including Marshall, as "cripples" (230). However, Fitzpatrick's discharge is rescinded immediately by Ewbank, who walks in on the departing Irishman. The tenting contractor appears to be unable to discharge any of his workers, regardless of their shortcomings:

EWBANK. And where the hell do you think you're going to? God Christ. Just look at the time. Knocking off and they've only been here half an hour.
FITZPATRICK. I've been fired.
EWBANK. Don't be so bloody silly. Get on with this bloody walling ... God damn and blast. (230)

Not only does the marriage appear to be facing difficulties, but the strong friendship between the two Irishmen can never again be the same. In the center of a challenging action, Marshall has shown that necessity will sever the tight bonds of the camaraderie he had previously enjoyed with Fitzpatrick; and Fitzpatrick, the more aggressive of the two, can never again take Marshall's loyalty for granted. The nature of their friendship will be permanently modified in this realization. Although this action is clearly peripheral to the principal activities of the play—the setting up of the tent and the marriage itself—it sharply echoes the impermanence of all relationships which is central to Storey's theme in this drama.[14]

Finally, the process of change, in its most poignant expression, is discovered in the complex layers of relationships among the male characters in the Ewbank family. Although Claire will marry, her children—if there are any—will not bear the Ewbank name, even if her marriage survives which, as we have seen, is most unlikely. That responsibility for family continuity falls upon the shoulders of Ewbank's son Paul, a wanderer, completely lacking in direction or ambition, and a most unlikely candidate to marry and to raise a family of his own. When Glendenning asks Paul what he does "for a living," Paul answers, "I'm kind of . . . I don't do anything at all as a matter of fact" (178). He later tells his mother that when the wedding is over he is going off but he has no idea where he is actually going (186).

Paul stands in very sharp contrast to his father, who takes pains to distinguish between himself and his son to Kay, his foreman. When Paul suddenly enters the work area he actually asks his father rather innocently if he had been working on setting up the tent. The question irritates Ewbank, whose pride as the contractor in over-all charge is piqued painfully, and he responds curtly to his son and then proceeds to further disparage Paul as he addresses Kay:

EWBANK. My work's done here. I'm a bloody artisan, I am. Not a worker. (*To Kay*) He's never believed that, Kay. And he's a . . . Well, I don't know what he is. He's supposed to be summat.
PAUL. (*To Kay*) I'm a drain on his pocket for one thing. He must have told you that. (176)

Paul is also sharply contrasted with his grandfather,[15] and if there is among these three generations of male Ewbanks a trajectory, it is pointing toward family dissolution, to the permanent severing of all family bonds, to the end of the Ewbank family line. The elder Ewbank appears lost in the past, in a world where he was at one time a maker of rope and prided himself on the excellence of his skills. Times have changed, and the corruption of the process of rope making—a symbol of the general corruption of the present times—has set in through the introduction of machines (203).[16]

So the line of the rope maker and the tent maker has finally descended upon Claire, who seems to be headed into a disastrous marriage, and upon Paul, who is quite literally heading nowhere. Both Old Ewbank and Ewbank himself have been hard working, dedicated, and successful, and they have both planted their feet, so to speak, solidly on the ground beneath them. At least, they always knew who they were, what they were doing, and where they were going. Ewbank made money and educated his children, but his children now appear to represent the end, not the continuation, of the family. As Old Ewbank and Ewbank were firm and solid men, the children appear insubstantial and vulnerable, ready to be blown away by whatever winds come rushing in their direction. As the tent is erected and reveals its beauty momentarily, so the Ewbank family prospered, revealing its substance, its strength, its expertise, but again, like the tent, only momentarily through the span of the two senior Ewbanks; as the tent is finally taken down and disappears offstage, so quite possibly will the Ewbanks as a family disappear, their continuity ending with Claire and Paul.

The sense of impending change and ultimate desolation is further underscored in the powerful closing imagery of the drama. Ewbank, alone upon the stage with his wife, wonders aloud as to what will happen to them now:

EWBANK. . . . What's to become of us, you reckon? (*Mrs. Ewbank looks at him, smiles, then shakes her head.*) Never do this again, you know.
MRS. EWBANK. No . . . (*She smiles.*)
EWBANK. Me heart wouldn't stand it. (246)

Finally they are called off by his elderly parents, who are preparing to depart from Ewbank's home. The closing, final image reverberates with Storey's theme of change and desolation:

(*They go.*
The stage stands empty: bare poles, the ropes fastened off.
The light fades slowly.)
                              CURTAIN
Indeed, there probably are, as Storey and other critics have suggested, many interpretations for this work[17], but the memory of the tent going up and coming down while the human activity on stage increases and decreases and while the difficulties and uncertainties facing the various characters in their relationships are suggested—all this surely establishes the thematic importance of impermanence and change, always unpredictable and always painful.

In November 1971, *The Changing Room* was produced at The Royal Court Theatre in London. Like its predecessor, *The Contractor* (1970), *The Changing Room* is an example of Storey's naturalism at its starkest expression and has to be one of the most unusual works of contemporary British drama.

As we have seen, *The Contractor* had a principal character, Ewbank, and a principal onstage event, the erecting and dismantling of the wedding marquee while the principal event of the drama, the wedding itself, occurred off-stage. *The Changing Room*, however, has no principal character and no central onstage event, although like *The Contractor*, its principal event, the rugby match, occurs offstage. As such, *The Changing Room* is an even more pronounced example of the Chekhovian concern with peripheral, day-to-day events in the lives of the characters on stage.[18]

We are simply in a changing room, the British equivalent of an American locker room, and in this room athletes arrive to prepare for a professional rugby match.[19] Their preparations before and after the match as well as the matter-of-fact activities of the team's various support individuals, ranging from Harry, the cleaner, to Sir Frederick Thornton, the chairman of the team, are the only events occurring on stage.

There is an injured player, Kendal, brought in from the playing field (138) while the game is in progress and momentarily treated before being dispatched to a hospital, but his appearance is presented in the routine flow of events facing a rugby team, a most brutal sport—the most brutally savage of all sports in Storey's judgment (Duffy 66)—and is no more central to the development of this drama than are the numerous, seemingly trivial events that clutter the busy stage: Harry's slipshod cleaning of the room (87) and intense paranoid fear of a projected Russian takeover of the entire world[20]; Kendal's purchase of an electric tool set (93), which provokes wide amusement on the part of his fellow players at Kendal's expense; the frequent application during the course of the entire drama of liniments and oils to salve the players' many minor injuries as well as the strapping of bandages to support injured muscles (94+); the rugby players placing bets on horse races (101) and one, Walsh, actually winning (164);

the chairman and his secretary drinking while the match is in progress (125) and later pretending to have actually seen the game (128); the players' horseplay before the game and their significantly more raucous horseplay in the communal bath after the match is completed (147+). Here there is an evenness about all activity, a sharp linearity that slices relentlessly throughout the play, leveling all characters and all action as part of a dramatic continuum, where no individual and certainly no event is of singular and commanding importance.

Although this may certainly sound static and undramatic, a series of disconnected trivial events, the effect is actually the reverse. *The Changing Room* is a transformation play like *The Contractor*. In *The Contractor* we see men erecting a tent and from their hard, meticulous labor, the final product, the wedding marquee, transforms itself into complex and richly textured levels of imagery from which profound implications arise; in the case of *The Changing Room*, the men themselves are the material out of which Storey constructs the play's central image: the team itself (Roberts 110–11). As such, the play is a further example of Storey's naturalistic style and may even surpass *The Contractor* in terms of its execution—in the application of the naturalistic idiom with its sparse diction and pyramiding of mundane encounters into a dramatic text that explores the process of separate individuals merging into a team, united in purpose, each individual subsumed by the collective dynamic mass. If the tent's erection and disassembly are central to *The Contractor,* so the fourteen separate athletes merging into a team and their subsequent dispersal as fourteen separate individuals, once the match is completed, are central to *The Changing Room.*

While watching *The Contractor* in performance on London's West End, Storey identified an image in his earlier play that led directly to the conception and the writing of *The Changing Room:* "The image of people coming into a room which was changed by them, and they in turn were changed . . . was curious and I thought of a changing room. . . . That came and I think I must have written it almost straightaway, over four or five days, I think it was" (Roberts 110).[21]

In this regard, Ronald Hayman who sees the drama as an example of "documentary realism," similar to "Zola's naturalism" suggests that Storey's training as a "visual artist" provided him with a "perceptual" focus that informs the dramatic construction of the play. It is neither the particular characters nor the particular events that are important, since they never achieve sufficient dramatic interest in themselves, but the view of the entire process developing, like the petals of a flower unfolding, a process that in the case of a changing room for a professional rugby team is "unfamiliar" to the majority of the members of the audience: "The wooden benches, the clothes pegs, the towels, the rugby boots . . . the male bodies in progressive stages of dressing and undressing and the physical actions, including massage." Actually, what we are seeing, Hayman maintains, is a "choreography of actions"[22] where the intentional absence of significant characters or events "helps to focus attention on the individual actions. As in looking at a representational painting, the spectator can concentrate on the quality of the art" (*British Theatre since 1953: A Reassessment,* 58).

It is, therefore, the dynamic mass, the congealing of all the disparate elements, so to speak, that is the focus as the various men bond into a team, play their match, and disperse: they enter the room as individuals, undress, and put on their uniforms, exiting the stage as a unified entity, a team. Once the match is completed, they again undress, bathe, and dress in their street clothes, returning to their individual selves. The transformation of the individual men into a unified team and their subsequent return as individuals has been completed.

In addition, Storey develops the twenty-two characters—the fourteen players, the two reserves, and six support personnel, including the team's aristocratic chairman (86)—with sharply drawn defining characteristics. There is here a very real Chekhovian[23] influence in the skillful depiction of a wide range of humanity. Each man stands out clearly and specifically, and the society that produced him can also be sharply inferred from his behavior in the changing room.[24]

Among the players there is Patsy who is first to arrive and first to leave after the game is over. Patsy is meticulous and "very well groomed, hair greased, collar of an expensive overcoat turned up" (88). He begins his preparation for the game while chatting with Harry (88–89). And then rather rapidly the remaining team members appear, all of whom converse with each other as well as with Harry, from the "easy going" Fielding, "a large, well-built man" (90) to Kendal, a typical Storey innocent, who gets his nose smashed during the game and has, according to the masseur Luke, "Been round half the teams i' the bloody league . . . one time or another" (142).

In sharp contrast to these men there is Trevor, "a studious-looking man," who is "a schoolmaster" (96)[25] and is married to a woman with a "university degree" (99) in economics, a fact that greatly amuses and provokes Walsh, the most raucous, rowdy, and defiant character among the players, who even acts rather aggressively toward Sir Frederick (157). Walsh is a kind of natural leader among the men, and his sense of humor is both appreciated and feared.[26] Quickly, the remaining players arrive, each preparing himself for the game. We are watching some sixteen men undressing and getting dressed in their uniforms and as one critic has observed: "The variety shown comes not from the fact that different things are being done, but that the same things are being done at different times" (Roberts 114). Thus, the undressing and dressing are an aspect of the drama's "choreography of actions"; this choreography of identical activity, each quite trivial in itself, contributes to the larger image developing on the stage—the image of a rugby team preparing for a game—and the image undeniably has the power of a representational painting which, as had been previously observed, is an aspect of Storey's "perceptual focus" in his training as a visual artist (*British Theatre since 1953: A Reassessment*, 58).

In addition to the players, there are the referee and the team's support staff (the cleaner, the trainers, the masseur, the secretary); and these men, like the players themselves, are working class, but Storey expands the range of class representation with the inclusion of Sir Frederick, the team's chairman, an aristocrat and a man of comparative affluence.   Interestingly, Sir Frederick wants to be very much a part of the hard, parochial world created by the players and is extremely friendly and patronizing toward the men around him.   For example, he even gently admonishes Harry for having addressed him by title: "Nay, no bloody titles here, old lad" (125).   Storey himself has noted that in the world of rugby in Yorkshire the puritanical element of molding all individuals into a collectivite unit is pervasive, "so that, for example, the rich in this region are relatively indistinguishable in appearance from the comparatively poor" ("Writers on Themselves" 160).[27]

Furthermore, there is in Storey's drama nothing remotely suggesting a political interpretation of class struggle or a protest against the inequitable conditions among the men who play rugby and those, like Sir Frederick, who actually employ them. Although very much a working-class playwright, Storey's representation of his characters does not grow out of a particular ideological focus, Marxist or otherwise, as the playwright's concern with Sir Frederick is purely with his situation as he relates to his players and to himself and not with his economic position as chairman of the team or his class separation from the men beneath him.[28]

For example, Sir Frederick's separation from the team that he wishes to be a strong part of is evidenced in part by his drinking while the game is in progress (124–26), and his subsequent praise for plays he never actually saw (131, 158). Moreover, Sir Frederick apparently suffers from an intense loneliness, a form of spiritual homelessness, that in the drama far transcends in importance his economic position in relationship to the players on his team. For example, Luke, the masseur, attempts to find out where Harry actually lives and what specific place the cleaner thinks is his real "home." To point out clearly what he means by a real "home," the masseur tells Harry that he has in fact discovered Sir Frederick late at night crouched and sitting alone in the stands surrounding the rugby field:

LUKE. . . . F'un him up here, you know, one night.
HARRY. What's that?
LUKE. Sir Frederick . . . Came back one night . . . Left me tackle . . . Saw a light up in the stand . . . Saw him sitting theer. Alone. Crouched up like that. (136)

To Luke, the real home for Sir Frederick, is the rugby field, and despite his wealth and influence he returns to the cold, empty stadium when he wishes to be alone. Of course, Harry misses the point entirely, arguing fiercely that Sir Frederick, in view of his position, "Can sit theer when he likes" and whenever "he likes" (136).[29]

The actual bonding of the individual men into a team begins with their undressing and dressing into uniforms, thereby discarding their individual clothing and with these items a measure of their individual identity; this process is then intensified with the referee's inspection of the entire team for weapons and their subsequent practice of certain key moves:

> TALLON *goes round to each player, examines his hands for rings, his boots for protruding studs; feels their bodies for any belts, buckles or protruding pads. He does it quickly; each player nods in greeting; one or two remain aloof.*
>
> As TALLON *goes round,* HARRY *comes back with the resin board and two rugby balls; sets the board on the table against the wall. The players take the balls, feel them, pass them around, lightly, casual.* (114)

This activity, while underscoring the danger involved in rugby, is the beginning of the process of unifying the team into a specific entity—a collective entity that will subsume the individual players on the team. Also, to a very large extent, the offstage activity of the game proceeding simultaneously with the actions occurring in the changing room itself expands both the element of excitement and the genuine danger facing the players. In effect, the audience is not only concerned with the "perceived space," the action unfolding on stage, but also with the "conceived space," the activity occurring in the stands surrounding the playing field in the so-called "unseen theatrical space" (Scolnicov 14).

These terms are useful, particularly in a play like *The Changing Room*, in explaining the complex relationship that occurs between the energy flowing back and forth, between what is actually seen and what is imaginatively conceptualized. Such a balance of activity between that which is seen and that which is conceptualized, with both events occurring simultaneously, helps to intensify the context of unification in which the individual players on stage merge into the collective entity they become. They are not only molded into the team by the ritualistic behavior on the stage—in uniform they even look alike— but also by the pressure flowing in upon them from the "theatrical space without":

The unseen theatrical space is no less real and dramatically important than the visible theatrical space. Actions of great moment like Macbeth's murder of Duncan, may take place off stage in which I propose to call *the theatrical space without* as opposed to *the theatrical space within*. The difference between them is the difference between perceived space and conceived space. Any play, or dramatic style, may be characterized by the particular balance it strikes between the theatrical space within and without and the relative meaning it attaches to them. In other words, far from being accidental or arbitrary, the articulation of the theatrical space is, at its best, an expression of the playwright's philosophical stance. (Scolnicov 15)

The team's warm-up, just before the men depart for the playing field, continues to develop the bonding that is occurring on stage. Crosby, the trainer, readies the team in last minute strategy and maneuvers (115) as the "roars" of the crowd are heard interspersed with "fanfare music"; and the men now have bonded collectively as they line up in a rigidly straight line behind Owens, their captain. Now, as a team, fired with the fierce energy to function as a single entity, the process of conversion of the many into the one has been completed (119). In effect, on the stage, the team, as a unit, is now the central image: it subsumes its individual components, the players themselves, as it, the team, has been defined and molded within the balance of the onstage and offstage activity.

There is, further, a ritual being performed as the men themselves produce from their own flesh the team that races out onto the playing field.[30] Hutchings identifies "three essential characteristics" that define the ritual in Storey's plays: "it is a *patterned, purposeful,* and *significant* (i.e., *status-affirming*) event" (*The Plays* 18). Hutchings further argues that there is an inventive quality in Storey where he is able to construct new rituals since "the traditional sources of secular rituals—the home and family—have been devalued"; and this enables the playwright to reinvent the "patterned" behavior necessary for ritual out of the closely dictated requirements of team sport, and to further identify such behavior with the central ritual of his play: the bonding of the men. This dramatic ritual, woven out of the elements of players' activities as they prepare to enter a match, makes *The Changing Room,* according to Hutchings, one of two plays that demonstrate the "most significant achievement" of Storey as an inventive dramatist (147).[31]

Finally, in *The Changing Room* there is an interesting connection to Performance Theater in general and to *Dionysus in 69* in particular[32] in that both plays specifically explore a birth ritual on stage: in *The Changing Room,* a team is born out of the flesh of the individual players; in *Dionysus in 69,* the god Dionysus is born within the individual performers themselves. As the individual rugby players become the team—and later, through immersion in the common bath, are restored to their individual selves—so the men and women in *Dionysus in 69* go through an elaborate birth ritual—a ritual that is documented with photographs of the original performance.

The women initially straddle the men as the latter lurch forth upon the floor, the resulting image representing a birth canal through which an embryo moves toward its exit from the womb as the god Dionysus. As a universality is achieved in *The Changing Room*—the many become the one—so a universality is achieved in *Dionysus in 69,* in that all, both the women and the men, are reborn as gods and proclaim their divinity to the audience. There is no question about the fascinating dramatic imagery produced in *Dionysus in 69* [33] as we witness the birth of a god. Storey is able to achieve a similar theatrical image—the birth of a team—in a scripted text without the elaborate staging involving audience participation and the physically demanding Grotowski exercises that were essential for the training of the actors.[34] In *Dionysus in 69*[35] the intention is to provide a ritualistic performance on the stage, while in Storey's play the ritual occurs naturally, flowing simply from the events without any self-consciousness on the part of the performers (Hutchings, *Casebook* 106). Although both works dramatize the ritual of transformation, Storey's technique is truly "invisible," in the manner described by Allott (*Life Class* 176-77), and performed without the rugby players' being conscious of the change, whereas The Performance Group's depiction of their ritual is obvious, self-conscious, and openly didactic.

This is not to compare the two works as dramatic experiences, since there are very real differences in depicting the bonding of men into a fiercely competitive team and the birth of a god, like Dionysus, but to emphasize the dramatic skill that Storey had developed by this time in his career—a skill enabling him to place before us, on a very crowded and noisy stage, a ritualistic experience that will resonate with its imagistic power long after the concerns of the individual rugby players are quietly forgotten.

In one other respect, Storey's written text is superior to the improvisational representation of ritual because *The Changing Room* can be—and in fact has been—produced repeatedly.[36] In contrast, The Wooster Group's text, although loosely written, is basically an extended improvisation on Arrowsmith's translation of Euripedes' *The Bacchae,* and as a performance piece it cannot be reproduced elsewhere because of the particular demands such a production requires—an unfortunate condition often found in performance theater generally.

For example, its set depended upon the complex structure erected in the Wooster Street Garage, an intricate network of towers and platforms that provided both seating for the audience and space for the actors, the use of which depended upon the arbitrary seating habits of the audience itself. Furthermore, the set, so central to this production, had to be molded to the spatial limitations of the Wooster Street Garage, where the performance took place; the actors themselves rotated in the various parts and their particular performance depended to a very large extent on the particular composition of the audience they were encountering each evening—they even had, as Richard Scheckner explains, different lines in response to different audience reactions (*Dionysus in 69* n. pag.).

Of course, like *The Changing Room, Dionysus in 69* can again be produced since its antiwar message (originally produced in response to the Vietnam conflict) is universal, but it would be a very different theatrical experience from the one originally produced. It would in effect be a different play, since there is no text; its content would depend upon the improvisational skills of the new actors and director as well as the circumstances of its production. It certainly may lend itself to a new and exciting theatrical event, but it is dramatically a "happening" (Hartnoll 103) rather than a scripted play.

There is a shift from the presentation of collective groups of men at work—tent erectors and rugby players—to the concentration on a single individual in Storey's *Life Class* (1975). While all three plays isolate the work experience, the first two focus on groups of individuals without a traditional protagonist, and the ultimate significance of the plays, as we have seen, emerge in the product of the labor: the tent and the team. In *Life Class* we again have a large group of people working, and, for the first time in Storey, women working as well as men—art students being instructed in a drawing class—but the focus in this drama has switched from the group and its product, presumably their drawings, to the instructor, Allott, and his interpretation of art: it is he and his language that become central to the play.

It is not simply that Storey lost interest in the individual characters in the play, for there is in *Life Class* further evidence of Storey's considerable ability to portray a wide range of humanity in brief dramatic strokes, not only among the art students themselves, but also among the college staff, including its eccentric principal Foley.[37] But the activities of the art students themselves—in this case, their drawing from the live model—never achieves the thematic richness that resonates in the imagery of the two previous dramas. More precisely, there is no complex dynamic event, like the raising of the tent or the bonding of the team, that emerges in *Life Class* and remains as an engaging symbol defying simple explanation or limited within the bounds of one critical interpretation.[38] Instead, we are left with language, an extended lecture, that is meant to interpret the significance of the limited action in the play and, apparently, to express in a wider context Allott's (and presumably Storey's) interpretation of the artistic event.

In effect, *Life Class* is a thesis drama on aesthetics, and while conceptually interesting, it is dramatically static and uncompelling. The events that Allott strives to interpret, namely his own sketching of a student who poses in the model's absence (214–16) as well as the sham attack upon

Stella, serve as events that illuminate the instructor's extended lecture on aesthetics.

As a result, the principal actions of the play—the sketch of Mathews and the attack on Stella—are stringently reductive: pedagogical visual aids that proceed to one and only one interpretation—Allott's—and even that interpretation, if actually given serious credence, would have forced Allott to remain as silent in his comments on the aesthetics of the events unfolding around him as he was noncommunicative in his sketching of Mathews (216). Despite his apparent sketching, his drawing pad remains empty. After Allott leaves the studio, Mathews, glancing at the empty pad, comments: "There's nothing there. . ." (216). Allott later explains his purpose: "There isn't any drawing . . . or, rather, the drawing was the drawing . . . perhaps you weren't aware" (219).

This drawing, where nothing is represented, is then explicated by Philips, another art instructor in the school, who seeks to assure Mathews, as well as us, presumably, that a great deal is going on since Allott is in fact a "purveyor of the invisible event . . . so far ahead of his time you never see it" (216).

Hutchings sees much here, despite the empty canvas, and argues that the art class, like the rugby players forming into a team, is in effect a ritual—"a patterned" event that is convened to create the beautiful, the aesthetic object, which is both elusive and mysterious (Hutchings, *Casebook* 33). Consequently, for Allott, "art has become . . . the surrogate religion of a desacralized world, and the classroom is the 'sanctified space' . . . in which the celebrants convene for an exalted purpose" (Hutchings, *Casebook* 111).

The problem with Hutchings's interpretation is that we can see and experience the fusion of players into a team without them ever explaining what is occurring; we cannot, on the other hand, see the significance of the empty canvas—it has to be explained to us and the explanation is tedious and pretentious. In addition, however much we wish to accept such an interpretation—to see in its emptiness a ritual accommodating a "desacralized world"—it becomes ludicrous when applied to the central event of *Life Class*: the sham rape of Stella.[39] Perhaps we can excuse Allott's lack of reaction. He appears immobilized, perhaps psychologically traumatized by his impending divorce (188). Perhaps Allott's inaction is an expression of the enervating influence of his own aesthetic—his need to distance himself from the events occurring about him.[40]   However, we cannot accept Stella's passivity to what has occurred, unless we assume she was in on the charade at its inception. There is no evidence in the drama to support this observation, and it is inconceivable that Stella, after the sham rape had been exposed, would return, without comment, to her posing as a model:

ALLOTT: .... I suppose the best solution ... Warren ... Mathews ... is to return to the job in hand . . . I to instruct; you to be instructed . . . Stella.
[Stella *looks round*:
Mathews *and* Warren *have returned to their donkeys: silence*
....Stella, *after a moment's hesitation, climbs up; glances at the students, disrobes, takes up her pose* ... (227-28).

Hutchings argues that Stella is involved in the "hoax" precisely because she returns to her pose (*Casebook* 113), but if she were, why did she not, at the very least, like Mathews and Warren, admit to her own complicity? Her silence as she resumes her pose suggests a profoundly apathetic individual curiously unaware of what has just occurred: she is neither amused nor offended. She simply "disrobes" and "takes up her pose."

Ironically, Storey in *Life Class,* violates his own aesthetic principle as expressed by Allott directly to his students:

ALLOTT: . . . a work of art can never exist. . . . It's not merely a conscious effort . . . it is, if one is an artist and not merely a technician . . . the gift, as it were, of song. . . . For, after all, a bird sings in its tree . . . but doesn't contemplate its song . . . similarly the artist sings *his* song, but doesn't contemplate its beauty, doesn't analyse . . . that is the task of the critic . . . That's the lesson we've been convened . . . to celebrate ... that we are life's musicians . . . its singers, and that what we sing is wholly without meaning . . . it exists, merely, because it is. (176–77)

Storey himself has made comments similar to Allott's, especially in regard to *The Contractor* (*A Reader's Guide* 430) where the playwright suggests that to insist on a critical interpretation would "shrink" a play rather than reveal its aesthetic power. The play, in other words, is its own meaning, or like Allott's bird singing, its own "song." Now Storey explicitly attempts to define the indefinable: the nature of the aesthetic in his drama. Even though he tells us it is "indefinable" and "invisible," he is still telling us, using language to explain what cannot be explained. No image, like the tent or the team, emerges for us to contemplate, and the action of the drama dissipates into critical commentary, with the play in the process collapsing as an artistic structure.

Moreover, despite Allott's disclaimers to the contrary, events in this play do happen: when Allott draws Mathews but produces nothing on his canvas, he is in fact producing an empty canvas; when Warren and Mathews attack Stella, despite their sexual simulation, an attack has nonetheless occurred. To define such events as "indefinable" is Allott's prerogative, but it does sound exceedingly precious and distanced from what is actually happening. Finally, and most importantly, to define the aesthetic experience as "indefinable" is to define it, and such a critical activity is the work of a "technician," a "critic," not an artist. The tent itself announces its own meaning without someone telling us that it is "indefinable."

The imagery of *The Contractor* and *The Changing Room* retains its power long after the details of the dramas themselves are forgotten. *Life Class*, unfortunately, leaves us with an argument, and the argument fades rather rapidly once the play has been read or viewed in production. After all, as Allott has said, "a bird sings in its tree . . . but doesn't contemplate its song" (176). Storey should have paid more attention to Allott's insight.

Storey's dramas set within the world of work demonstrate his basic aesthetic theory. The play has to work initially on the "purely literal level" and the interpretation of that image projected by the drama is left to the readers or viewers (*Retreats* 35). Critical commentary is, as Allott tells us, deadly, for the play is both its own beauty and its own complex meaning. *The Contractor* and *The Changing Room* are dramatic examples of Storey's theory. They are naturalistic works developed upon numerous, seemingly trivial events, exploring often in minute detail the world of work, and are constructed without principal characters or principal events; yet both works produce dramatic images that suggest an array of complex interpretations. Although *Life Class* also explores the world of work, it does so by explicitly stating the playwright's aesthetic. As such, *Life Class* is a statement of David Storey's artistic principles, but it fails as a drama intended to demonstrate those principles upon the stage.

NOTES

1. It is well known that Storey studied art and played professional rugby, but he was also employed for a time as an erector of tents like the men in *The Contractor* and the novel *Radcliffe* (Gindin 502).

2. Nevertheless in *The Changing Room* activities involving the players' support personnel—the cleaner, the trainers as well as the club's secretary and chairman—occur on stage simultaneously with the match, noises of which intrude upon the stage intermittently from the cheering of fans outside. In *The Contractor* the wedding occurs between acts 2 and 3.

3. An example of this form of dramatic construction carried to its most logical—or perhaps most absurd—limit is Israel Horovitz's "Stage Directions" (1977). In Horovitz's play, the stage business is the sole mode of communication—the characters literally speak the stage business and only the stage business—and despite the bizarre and jarring effect of such dialogue, the play in performance achieves a rather chilling effect, even if it is ultimately more gimmick than drama.

4. The white table at the end of *The Contractor* that produces the imagistic energy to compose *Home* is noted frequently in Storey commentary, but Storey himself gives the most direct representation of this creative event: *"The Contractor* was written immediately after *Arnold Middleton* had been on at the Court, and ... I was struck by the image of the white table at the end. . . . [A]nd perhaps two or three weeks later I sat down one morning and thought of the table sitting by itself and thought 'Well that's the beginning of something' and wrote a description of a metalwork table sitting by itself on a stage with two white chairs, bring on a chap after a little while—somebody has to appear" (Qtd. in *The Royal Court Theatre: 1965-1972* 107-108).

5. In the language of semiotics, the tent can be identified as an example of "metonomy," a rhetorical figure that represents "the substitution of cause for effect or of one item for something contiguous to it" like "the White House . . . for The President of the United States" (Elam 28). Hence, the tent represents an inherently impermanent structure, which does not bode well for the upcoming nuptials.

6. Storey's complex naturalistic plays like *The Contractor* are best approached from the semiotic perspective recently elaborated upon by Martin Esslin: "There can be agreement, by exact analysis, of what happens . . . on the purely factual, denotational level. . . . The theatre is a simulacrum—at its highest level, ordered and elevated to the status of art—of the real world and real life. That is why Antonin Artaud called his book *The Theatre and Its Double*. The theatre . . . is too complex to be capable of being reduced to a language with its predetermined rules of grammar and signification. Although drama uses many languages and signifying systems, it is the double of life itself. . . . That is why on any level, but especially on the highest plane of the hierarchy of meanings, the anagogic, a dramatic performance transcends any attempts at being reduced to anything so mundane as a single definable and generally valid meaning" (17–76).

7. See, for example, Carlson's discussion of architectural semiotics (*Theatre Semiotics* 42–43). The tent in Storey's play, however basic, is an architectural structure, and as such it announces its own impermanence.

8. Peter Brook notes that in drama "what remains, after the particular plot elements are forgotten, is the play's 'central image,' which burns a 'silhouette' into the minds of the viewers, and it is this image . . . that retains the drama's complexity and communicates its 'essence' " (136).

9. See Eccl. 1.14, King James Version: "I have seen all the works that are done under the sun; and, behold, all is vanity and vexation of the spirit."

10. See, for example, Nightingale, who argues that despite the considerable effort in constructing the tent its purpose is "essentially impermanent and dubiously useful" (430).

11. Ewbank is a minor character in the novel *Radcliffe* (1963). As in the play, he is a tenting contractor who employs both Leonard and Tolson, the two principal characters of the novel, to erect tents. This is another example of the same character appearing in Storey's plays and novels.

12. Maurice's desire for some alcohol may not be all that innocent or celebratory; he may in fact have a drinking problem. At the conclusion of act 2, Claire reminds him rather pointedly to try to "stay sober" for the wedding ceremony (216). This unpleasant circumstance, introduced

quietly, is further evidence that the intended marriage will have its serious difficulties.

13. Glendenning is similar in his guileless behavior to the actions of Alfred in *Home*, Kendal in *The Changing Room*, and Albert in *The Farm* (1973). All of these unsophisticated characters represent men who are innocent of treachery. They are simply present as basic and uncomplicated individuals whose innocence contrasts sharply with the behavior of the other characters in their respective plays.

14. Storey's ability to etch briefly the defining characteristics of the various workmen and to explore their day-to-day concerns as the tent is erected is an example of what Susan Rusinko identifies as the specific Chekhovian influence upon Storey—an ability that enables the playwright to focus upon "peripheral activities surrounding a major event, rather than the event itself " (112).

15. Old Ewbank, the grandfather, is clearly modeled on Storey's own grandfather about whom he had written a poem "Grandfather" in his autobiographical *Storey's Lives*. Like Old Ewbank, Storey's grandfather had "manufactured ropes" but gave up his craft when ropes were "made of metal, spliced by machine" (8).

16. Old Ewbank is like Harry, the cleaner in *The Changing Room*. Both men live locked in memories of a better world where they were nourished by a purity of activity that is no longer present: real rope was made and real rugby players engaged each other in real sport. Today the world is shoddy and fake, and the impurity that so troubles Old Ewbank is now represented most directly by his grandson Paul.

17. See, for example, Pearce who argues that "the tent symbolizes the struggle to make a world of illusions and to keep it up" (55); and Storey's assertion that the play may be "a metaphor for artistic creation: all the labour of putting up this tent, and when it's there, what good is it" (qtd. in John Russell Taylor, *The Second Wave: British Drama of the Sixties* 145).

18. Chekhov defined the new form of naturalism that Storey later employs as follows: "The demand is made that the hero and the heroine . . . should be dramatically effective. But in real life people do not shoot themselves, or hang themselves or fall in love . . . every minute. They spend most of their time eating, drinking ... talking nonsense" (qtd. in Rosen, *Plays of Impasse* 129.)

19. As Martha Duffy learned in her interview, "sport" for David Storey "is a form of work that goes beyond the personal and becomes, like art, something transcending, both to the performer and the observer" (69). William Hutchings also suggests a strong parallel between sport and theater: "Almost all sports events are inherently theatrical—conflicts (*agons*) that are 'staged' in especially equipped arenas by 'players' whose performances are assessed by knowledgeable but nonparticipating audiences" (*The Plays* 161.)

20. In fact, Harry explains to Patsy, the first player who has arrived to prepare for the match, that the Russians are responsible for the frigid outside weather, which is actually mixed with a "chemical" designed to control the minds of all in the world (89); indeed, as Harry continues, within "twenty-five years no one country on earth'll not be communist" (90).

21. Interestingly, *Home,* as we have seen, was inspired by the white table left at the end of *The Contractor* (Findlater 113) while *The Changing Room* was inspired by *The Contractor* because of the manner in which space is transformed by its occupants who in turn are transformed by the very space that they have changed (Roberts 110).

22. Storey himself in commenting on the first day of rehearsals for *The Changing Room* underscores the choreographic elements of his work by observing that "the play is rather like a ballet and the only way you can start working is to get the people on the stage and start juggling. The movements are not generally dictated by the lines, although you have to put people in the right relationship in order for the lines to work " (Roberts 119).

23. For example, Harry the cleaner is strikingly similar to Chekhov's Firs. Like Harry, who operates outside of the flow of the rugby game and indulges in his memory of the past when rugby was a pure sport, so Firs in *The Cherry Orchard* operates at the periphery of the Ranevskaya family and also indulges in memories of a pure past: "In times gone by, why generals, barons and admirals came to our dances, but now we send for the post office clerk and the stationmaster—and even they come against their will"(197). Consider Harry's similar complaint as he compares the rugby players of today with their counterparts in the past: "Players? . . . Couldn't hold a bloody candle ... In them days they'd do a sixteen-hour shift, *then* come up and lake [play]. ... Nowadays: it's all machines ... and they're still bloody

puffed when they come up o' Sat'days. Run round youn field a couple of times: finished. I've seen 'em laking [playing] afore with broken arms, legs broke . . . shoulders. . . . Get a scratch today and they're in here, flat on their bloody backs: iodine, liniment, injections" (125). Interestingly, both Firs and Harry owe their primary allegiance to those who employ them: Firs to the Ranevskaya family, to whom he is most solicitous and dedicated, and Harry to Sir Frederick, the owner of the team. When Harry is chided by Luke, the masseur, for never watching a rugby match, Harry fires back: "I work for Sir Frederick, lad: for nob'dy else" (137).

24. J. W. Lambert has written that at the play's conclusion "one feels one could write short character sketches of all twenty-two participants and a passably accurate summary of the sort of world they live in, its grimy, demanding jobs, bleak industrial landscapes and starved culture" (14). Indeed, as Storey himself has said, this is an inherently violent sport (Duffy 66); and that rugby "is inherently puritanical with its puritanical distrust of the individual, the loner; as a result, each individual must merge himself ... within the group's identity ("Writers on Themselves" 160).

25. Trevor may very well be modeled on Storey himself, since the playwright at one time taught in a secondary school (Gindin 502). Also Trevor, because of his education, is frequently treated as an outsider, a situation that recalls Storey's own experiences during his playing days while he, alone among his teammates, was also an art student at the Slade ("Writers on Themselves" 159-161).

26. Although Storey has documented his painful isolation in the anti-intellectual and anti-artistic world of the rugby player ("Writers on Themselves" 159–62), there is considerable reason to believe that Storey himself admires these rough and extremely physical men. There is about the rugby players, regardless of their crudeness and puritanical morality, something very admirable in their simplicity and sheer physicality, in their power and evident willingness to engage in a dangerous sport. This is , of course, paradoxical, but it is nonetheless evident in Storey's persistent concern with such men and his evident pleasure at portraying them in their fierce energy. Obviously, the physical lives of the miner and the rugby player have a powerful appeal, as physical power previously appealed to a fellow Yorkshire man, D. H. Lawrence. This, of course, becomes even more evident when

we examine Storey's family dramas in chapter 4, where the children of miners who have been educated into professions, more often than not, find their lives empty, unfulfilling, and purposeless. Perhaps the cause for these feelings is the absence of the very intense excitement that the danger of the physical world provides. Storey may not particularly like the rugby players and certainly can fault them for their puritanical views on life and art and their intellectual limitations; but he clearly admires their physicality and courage, and this is demonstrated through their energy upon the stage and throughout Storey's entire career as a dramatist and novelist.

27. This observation describes Ewbank quite accurately as well. In his gruff and direct behavior, he is very much like the men he employs.

28. Lindsay Anderson has said of Storey's plays that "they aren't what the bourgeoisie—and very often the working class themselves—expect working-class plays to be. They're not plays of protest; they're not plays of scandal or squalor; they are subtle, poetic plays" (qtd. in Mather 5).

29. The portrait of Harry is particularly complex. Even though he is employed by a professional rugby team, he has never seen a rugby match (136); however, on two occasions in the play when he is alone (137, 145), he turns on the Tannoy, the loudspeaker, to listen to the precise, play-by-play descriptions of the match, a clear indication of his deep involvement with the sport. Obviously Harry is a fan, despite his disclaimers about the sorry state of contemporary rugby (125), but he cannot let his interest be known to the players themselves.

30. Storey himself identifies an interesting parallel between the players on the team and the actors themselves. He sees the theatrical experience itself as "a religious experience," since the actors must bond as a theatrical entity in order to do the play, even though they do not know each other personally. Once the play is over, the actors leave, each to his own pursuits, just as the players on the team, once the match is over, disconnect from each other to return to their former lives (Gussow 14).

31. *The Contractor* is the second example of Storey's most inventive use of ritual dramatization (Hutchings, *The Plays* 147).

32. The text for this production in 1970 is essentially improvisations made by individual members of The Performance Group on William Arrowsmith's translation of Euripides' *The Bacchae* with

copious editorial comments by Richard Scheckner, explaining the requirements for the production and the evolving conception. The piece has been published with photographs of the performance but unfortunately it does not contain pagination.

33. See, in the early pages of the text, the section devoted to the birth ritual and the accompanying photographs by Frederick Eberstadt (*Dionyus in 69* n. pag.)

34. This information, including the construction of the set and the involvement of the audience, is provided by Richard Scheckner in running editorial comments on the text; furthermore, the photographs also give evidence to the extremely complex nature of this performance (*Dionysus in 69* n. pag.)

35. For an interesting negative reaction to *Dionysus in 69,* see Lillian Feder who argues that although the work's "aim was to unite actors and audience in a communal rite," the unfortunate result was a "pseudo-rite" and "narcissistic exhibition of personal grievances and grandiose fantasies" (243–44).

36. *The Changing Room* opened at The Royal Court in November, 1971, and then transferred to the Globe (London); it was subsequently produced at the Morosco Theatre in New York in 1973 where it won the New York Drama Critics Award and was also nominated for a Tony Award as best play.

37. Foley is an excellent example of Storey's use of the same character in a novel and a play. He appears initially as R. N. Wilcox in the novel *A Temporary Life* (1973) and resurfaces as Foley a year later in *Life Class:* both men are the heads of art colleges for whom the principal characters work; each argues passionately that good eating habits are essential for good artistic production; both are extremely parsimonious, going so far as to steal coal for their personal use from their respective institutions; and both dismiss the principal character from his job as an art instructor. Finally, as Phyllis Randall has pointed out, there is even a "key incident" repeated in both the novel and the play: "the exchange of urine specimens for objects d'art" (254).

38. Janelle Reinelt, in her unpublished doctoral dissertation, argues that Stella, the model, becomes "generalized Woman as well as particular Stella" (165); as such, Stella is the "prominent physical image . . . equivalent to the tent in *The Contractor*" (167). Of course, there is no question that individuals, like Vladimir and Estragon, can

resonate with complex levels of meaning, but this is certainly not true for Stella. She is, as a character, rather severely delimited in Storey's depiction: she is perky, capable of verbally dueling with the off-color comments of the art students, and friendly and understanding towards Allott. In fact, she is rather plainly drawn, and never achieves the complexity that the tent achieves in *The Contractor*. We remember the tent and puzzle over its meaning; no such situation arises in our encounter with Stella.

39. For a sharply contrasting view, see Quigley who, while condemning Allott for not intervening, sees the attack as a crucial emblematic statement: "The frantic sexual embrace of the model and the student is a superb emblematic image of the play's thematic concern with the separability of life and art, and with the issue of whether life (the nude model) circumscribes art, or whether art (the male art student) circumscribes life" (275).

40. Quigley suggests that Allott's "refusal to intervene and protect the female model is an attempt to preserve his disinterested stance as an artist and an observer" (275).

4

FAMILY PLAYS

David Storey has written five plays that pierce the notion
that the family is a haven against the dangers of the outside world. Three of the plays focus upon the difficult relationships between working-class parents and their university-educated children as well as the equally difficult
relationships among the siblings themselves: *In
Celebration* (1969), *The Farm* (1973), and *The March o n
Russia* (1989). Two of these plays, *In Celebration* and *T h e
March on Russia*, are, as we shall see, companion pieces
and, despite changes in family name, examine the same
set of parents as they evolve over a period of twenty
years—the Shaws in *In Celebration* are in effect the
Pasmores in *The March on Russia*. [1]

The Farm (1973) is also a working-class family play
with a different dramatic focus. In *In Celebration* and
The March on Russia the bitterness is centered in the
children—more particularly Andrew in *In Celebration*
and Wendy in *The March on Russia*—and is exacerbated by
the unjustness of their parents' suffering to provide them

with university educations and middle-class status. However, in *The Farm*, it is the father, Slattery,[2] who expresses the drama's anger and bitterness towards his educated children, and even on occasion towards his own wife who is attempting to elevate herself beyond her class limitations with night classes in "Sociology. Psychiatry. *Anthropology*" (37). Like his children, Slattery's wife in her academic pursuits has become a cultural class enemy within her own family. She has separated herself from her husband, a man engaged in the physically exhausting, yet necessary labor of farming. Compared to his children whom he views as unproductive and pretentious and his wife whom he believes is "daft"(6) for going to night school, Slattery sees himself as the only one in the household who has maintained a genuine level of dignity. He alone functioned in the "real" world through physical labor, or "work" which is, he claims, "the only bloody thing that's real" (47).

Moreover, *The Farm* projects, as we shall see, an image of the family as evolving into something unnatural, "an animal with seven heads" (26), and ultimately disappearing through the children's failure to marry and produce children of their own. At the same time, of the three plays, despite its dark image of the ultimate disintegration of the family itself, *The Farm* creates the most humorous character, the irascible Slattery, who is intimidating, bombastic, and singleminded in his respect for physical labor (6), but his "bark," as Slattery himself points out, is much louder than his proverbial bite (52).

The two remaining family dramas, *Mother's Day* (1976) and *Early Days* (1980), reflect obvious literary influences that indicate Storey's willingness to experiment in dramatic structure and tone. However, despite the absence of class conflict within these dramas, the projected images of the family are equally bleak. *Mother's Day* is clearly a farce, very much conceived and executed under the influence of Joe Orton—in particular, Orton's *Entertaining Mr. Sloan* (1964). The family here is magnified through a farcical lens into a virtual lunatic asylum in which family and nonfamily members alike engage in a Byzantine chain of highly improbable criminal events. *Early Days* is a brief and dark Pinteresque vision of the family, depicted as ultimately treacherous, particularly in its suffocating grip on its aging and now dependent patriarch, Sir Richard Kitchen. Moreover, in *Early Days* Storey extends his dramatic examination of the family beyond that of the working-class family, to the world of Sir Richard, a former politician and a man of comparative affluence.[3] In this drama Storey focuses upon the ultimate human failure: never knowing anyone else. As we grow older, like Sir Richard, the realization arrives with stinging clarity that those closest to us, the very members of our own family, are essentially unknowable. To the elderly, like Sir Richard, family life becomes a web of treachery in which personal freedom is lost and one is maintained "on sufferance" (38).

However, it is best to begin our discussion of Storey's family dramas with *In Celebration* (1969) and its companion piece *The March on Russia* (1989). *In Celebration* begins Storey's close examination of family life, and *The March on Russia* completes that particular examination, as both dramas are about the same set of parents, even though there are gender differences among the children.[4]

Both plays are clearly autobiographical in setting, the dramas occuring within the homes of coal miners, an environment identical to David Storey's. In a reflective and poignant moment, the three Shaw brothers in *In Celebration*, now all university educated, recall with a sharp sense of distance and detached humor the deprivations of their childhood:

ANDREW. You forget, don't you, what a primitive place this really
is. . . . we never had toothpaste at home. . . . We all used to clean our
teeth with salt. (*Laughs*) Three little piles on the draining board every morning, when we came down.
STEVEN. We never had any cakes either. Do you remember that?
There was a jam tart, or one piece of a sponge roll, for tea on Sunday.
COLIN. And old Steve there used to stand at table because we only had
four chairs. (38)

Similarly the Pasmore children comment on the painful
circumstances of their own childhood, particularly in
viewing the suffering of their father:

COLIN. Remember when he [the Father] got a septic thigh? A cut that
became infected. In the hospital they said they'd have to cut his leg
off. One last chance they said was to put on boiling fomentations. I'd
just left him, after a visit. I heard him scream. . . . "If he can suffer like
that," I thought, "I have to work much harder."
EILEEN. I remember him going to work with ulcers on his legs.
WENDY. He treated them with onions.
EILEEN. The smell! (28)

Both plays also reflect Ibsen's technique in exposing
character, particularly in the peeling "of layer after layer"
of "defensive psychological armor" to enable the playwright to penetrate deeply into the matrix of "molten
family relations" (Billington, "A Play Worth Having"
16A).

In explaining why Andrew does not confront his
mother in *In Celebration*, Storey comments on his own
similarity to Ibsen in revealing character, but notes an important difference from the Norwegian playwright in
dramatic strategy:

If you compare it [*In Celebration*] with Ibsen in terms of approaching
emotional realities, Ibsen is writing about before the explosion has
happened, the bomb is festering away inside. *In Celebration* is after

the bomb's shown what it can do. It's not a question of stripping off hypocrisies ... but of realizing that once you have, there's nothing much really there afterwards. ("Conversations with David Storey" 49)

Storey here is defending himself by referring to what many have seen as an obvious defect in the play: the failure of Andrew to directly confront his mother, the principal object of his anger and resentment.

Even Storey's own brother, Anthony Storey, himself a novelist, identifies the lack of confrontation in *In Celebration* as the principal defect in the play. In Anthony Storey's novel *Brothers Keepers*, he has the entire family visit a production of *In Celebration* (entitled *The Family* in the novel), and the principal character, Tony, points out that in the drama "there's always the promise of something exploding" but the dramatic confrontation that would "expose the pretenses" in the family never occurs—except, in a rather unusual manner, in brother Anthony's novel, where the mother is reduced to tears and the father is deeply angered over the presentation of "family secrets" on the stage (*Brothers Keepers* 64–65).

Nevertheless, Storey believes that his technique demonstrates the effects of what has happened within the family after the so-called explosion has occurred, while Ibsen is interested in stripping away the "hypocrisy" prior to the central event that shatters and exposes the "hypocrisies" of the family members.

Interestingly, similarities occur in each of these dramas, *In Celebration* and *The March on Russia*, that suggest rather convincingly that David Storey has revisited the same set of parents. The coal miners, Harry Shaw and Tommy Pasmore, suffer an identical distressing paradox as fathers: they both want their children to enter professions and elevate themselves into middle-class status, yet, at the same time, they find such lifestyles unproductive, pompous, and profoundly distasteful. To both Shaw and Pasmore, the very sight of middle-class people provokes either humor or rage.

Chatting with his friend Reardon, Harry Shaw comments on the other diners in the restaurant at the Hotel Excelsior where his fortieth anniversary dinner was held:

REARDON. Captains of industry, Harry.
SHAW. They were. They were. You're right. Mill-owners. Engineering managers. Leaders of our imports . . . exports. Never done a day's work in their bloody lives. . . (62). [5]

Here of course the reaction is to the unproductive lives of successful people—they have "never done a day's work"; there is humor in these comments, but the reaction covers a darker and deeper anger at the very injustice of the class system itself. Those men and women who reap the material benefits of the system actually lead unproductive lives; yet it is precisely these lifestyles that Shaw and Pasmore wish their children to pursue. Steven, Shaw's most intellectually promising son, who as a young student possessed the greatest contempt and "venom" for middle-class respectability (40–41), sums up the irony that is central to his father's dilemma:

STEVEN: The funny thing is . . . he [Shaw] . . . raised us to better things which, in his heart—my dad—he despises even more than Andrew ... I mean, his work actually has significance for him ... while the work he's educated us to do . . . is nothing . . . at the best a pastime, at the worst a sort of soulless stirring of the pot. (84)

Similarly, Tommy Pasmore in *The March on Russia* is confronted by his daughter Wendy over his "bad" behavior in the restaurant among the "well-dressed" diners during his sixtieth wedding anniversary luncheon:

WENDY. You were bad enough in the restaurant, Dad.
PASMORE. Can't stomach well-dressed people.
EILEEN. You're well-dressed.
PASMORE. I'm only well-dressed when I'm going out with you.   (36)

The fathers have been so hardened by the rigors and deprivations of the coal mine that the very sight of middle-class people—their comparative physical softness and their intellectual and artistic interests—drives them into a rage.[6] To them, at the very least, such lives do not entail the dignity of true physical labor—these middle-class people who work with their minds do not produce anything of value. They do not even produce coal. At the same time, however, the thought of their own sons descending into the coal pits is the powerful motivation driving the men to the extremity of their sacrifice. Paradoxically, of course, the fruits of their sacrifice as coal miners—middle-class respectability—is a lifestyle neither Harry Shaw nor Tommy Pasmore can tolerate.

Both fathers are also seen by their children as men who have been decent and honorable as husbands, but have nevertheless been unjustly vilified by their spouses for the meanness of their circumstances as coal miners. Both mothers are excessively tidy and persistent in their petty objections to their husbands' personal habits. This indeed rankles both Andrew in the early play and Wendy in the later play, as both comment sharply on the injustice and ingratitude that their mothers' behavior has promoted within the family.

For example, the mothers in both plays attempt to conceal the truth about their own humble backgrounds while maintaining a condescending attitude of social superiority toward their miner-husbands. In *In Celebration* Mrs. Shaw rankles with bitterness every time her husband refers to her father as a "pig breeder" while she maintains he was a "small holder" (20); in *The March on Russia*, Mrs. Pasmore maintains her father had been a farrier who was out of work as a result of a wound in the Boer War, which explains why they spent time in a home for the poor, "the workhouse" (27). Nonetheless, neither woman will openly confess to the deprivations of their own family backgrounds.

Moreover, in *In Celebration*, the father is depicted as a man who has been forced into marriage because he had in a moment of passion impregnated the mother. In Andrew's view, the father has paid the horrendous price of involvement in a loveless union for his entire life as a result of his sexual transgression—the Shaws' first son Jamey was born three months after their marriage (45), convincing proof to Andrew, at least, that the marriage was forced upon his father. In *The March on Russia*, Wendy sharply reminds her mother that her life as a housekeeper, however humble, was comparatively easy and considerably safer when compared with the dangers her husband has faced as a coal miner (45).

The pettiness of the mothers' behavior is further underscored in both dramas when it is measured by the children's genuine concern over the fathers' health. For example, Harry Shaw who chokes on coal dust has silicosis and a heart problem (13); similarly Tommy Pasmore has "pneumoconiosis" (10). [7]

In addition, the children's interest in seeing the father retire to the seaside in *In Celebration*, for which the most affluent, Colin Shaw, a labor negotiator in the auto industry, offers to arrange (14), is in fact satisfied in *The March on Russia*. Colin, now a Pasmore and a university professor as well as a successful author (19), has placed his aging parents in a retirement cottage, the setting of the drama.

Even the aging of the characters in both plays corresponds accurately to the passage of twenty years—the actual period of time between both productions, 1969 and 1989. In *In Celebration*, the Shaws are in their sixties; in *The March on Russia*, the Pasmores are in their eighties. Moreover, the very dramatic action that initiates both plays is identical: homecomings to celebrate the wedding anniversary of their parents.[8] In *In Celebration*, the children arrive to celebrate their parents' fortieth anniversary; in *The March on Russia*, they arrive to celebrate their sixtieth. In both plays, the family goes out to expensive restaurants—each time the bill is picked up by Colin—the actual celebration occurring offstage during the intermission.[9]

Most importantly, however, the expected confrontation between Andrew, the ex-solicitor turned artist, and his mother, which never actually occurs in *In Celebration*, resurfaces in *The March on Russia*. This confrontation now occurs between Wendy, who has replaced Andrew in the earlier play as the sibling most angered over the treatment of her father. She, admittedly with less anger and energy than Andrew had earlier displayed, finally confronts her mother over the treatment of her father:

WENDY. He was a very good father.
MRS. PASMORE. You don't know the half of it. You don't know your father, love, at all.
WENDY. I know he coughed his guts out at the coal-face for the better part of fifty years. What did you do, Mother?
MRS. PASMORE. She always had a vicious streak. (*To Eileen*) You can see what I had to put up with. If she gets it from anyone it's not from me.
WENDY. Your life was no harder, Mother, than that of many woman, and a good deal easier than most. (45)

Of course, Wendy's anger is not as harsh as Andrew's, who tells his father that he has "enshrined" his wife in "adoration"—which she most certainly does not deserve.

"You owe her *nothing*," Andrew shouts (81). Nevertheless, Wendy at least confronts her mother directly, unlike Andrew who deflects his comments toward his brothers and his father when the latter is much too drunk to hear clearly what is being said (79). In effect, Wendy, some twenty years later, is articulating the resentment that Andrew sublimated in the earlier play—and directing it at its proper target, her mother.

It could also be argued that Wendy is very much a recreation of Andrew, despite the difference in gender. Apart from the similarity in their views toward their fathers and their resentment at the ingratitude of their mothers, there are also similar cynical attitudes toward their current professional situations in life. For example, Andrew has given up the law (23), and Wendy has given up her position in politics (15). Andrew, who has now become an artist, responds cynically to his mother's request that he define the nature of his own painting which he claims contains "not a sign of human life" (24), while Wendy similarly shows a contemptuous attitude toward politics as well as towards her dismissal as a member of the Labour Party (18). Even the gender difference is minimized as the older sister Eileen tells Wendy that both of them should indeed have been men (29). It is amusing to think that Storey actually has Andrew return some twenty years later as Wendy to finally chastise the mother over her condescending and cruel treatment of their father.

There are, however, important differences between the two plays, particularly in the manner in which the children confront each other—the Shaw brothers in *In Celebration* and Colin Pasmore and his sisters Wendy and Eileen in *The March on Russia*. In each drama, the children measure the value of their own lives against the sacrifices of their parents. In the earlier play, however, the feelings are often acrimonious and intense and loom dan-

gerously close to boiling over into fierce, physical confrontation, particularly between the artist Andrew and his
relatively affluent brother Colin, who is viewed to some
extent as a class traitor for mediating in behalf of man-
agement with the workers in the auto industry (36).
Andrew is clearly a young and very angry man, much under the influence of John Osborne's Jimmy Porter.[10]
Unlike Jimmy Porter, however, Andrew is attacking the
very class into which he has gained entrance as a result of
his education—his anger is directed towards himself and
those like him who have been elevated into the middle
class only to find that world unrewarding. He believes,
despite the privilege of his education, he has inherited
"nothing" (81).

In the latter play, however, the children themselves
are now middle-aged, and are considerably more reflective
about their own lives and the lives of their parents.[11] The
anger and energy of the earlier play is indeed muted, perhaps through the children's suffering and disappoint-
ments. For example, Wendy has never had any children,
despite her strong desire for them and her numerous attempts to conceive. She tells her sister Eileen what she
has endured:

WENDY. Alkaline douches. I'm afraid didn't do the trick. Neither
did sexual positioning, temperature graphs or artificial insemination—
techniques which, in my case, came too late. Ten years younger . . . I
might have had a child. (46)

Wendy's attitude toward marriage and her impending
divorce is also indicative of an individual who has given
up entirely on the notion of family as a necessary and de-
sirable institution. Whatever happens now, Wendy will
accept the consequences and direct her own life as she sees
fit. "Husbands" and the institution of the family itself are
"nothing at all" to Wendy (46).

Although Wendy's attitude may suggest a defeated individual who is incapable of getting on with her life, the opposite is clearly true. Unlike Andrew, who expresses impotent rage at the injustice of his family's situation, particularly his father's, Wendy is capable of acting decisively to correct impending difficulties. At the end of *In Celebration*, Andrew on the following morning cannot even tell his mother the truth about the nature of the argument between him and his brothers. He claims, rather weakly, that it was all about "politics" (94).

Wendy, on the other hand, at the end of *The March on Russia*, intercedes on her father's behalf. Pasmore has been threatened with a criminal action for stealing from a local shopkeeper and fears that he will go to "prison" (48).[12] Wendy, however, consoles her father and assures him that she will deal with the shopkeeper before she returns home (56). As she is capable of directly confronting her mother, so is she capable of acting on behalf of her father. Andrew's rage, ineffective and misdirected, has been transmuted into Wendy's focus and capacity to act decisively when such action is necessary.

Further, although both plays are initiated by events intended to celebrate married life, what they in fact celebrate is the pain of "guilt-ridden marriage," as one critic noted about *In Celebration* (Wertheim 159). The drama begun in the earlier play is completed some twenty years later, both plays presenting a continuity of pain, disillusion, and despair within the Shaw and Pasmore families.[13]

Unlike Shaw and Pasmore, Slattery, in *The Farm* (1973), does not want his children to seek professions and enter the world of the middle class. Since he is a farmer, he is exceedingly familiar with hard work, but his view of such labor is that it is the only thing worth doing. Quite unjustly, Slattery maintains, society gives all the credit to "them that do damn all" while those, like himself, who actually do the work "get no attention"; and this injustice in the appreciation of human labor is due simply to defects in "human nature" (36). As a consequence, Slattery does not want his children to succeed in a middle-class lifestyle that he personally detests in order to avoid the rigor of physical labor. He views his daughters' profession of teaching as unproductive and basically a form of non-labor.

When Slattery's wife defends her son against the charge of habitual indolence, she points out that Arthur has had "jobs" and "even taught" at one time. This information sends Slattery into an amusing tirade on the profession of education:

SLATTERY. Taught? Couldn't teach my bloody felt cap, I'm telling you. And that's nothing personal, mind. It's just a statement of bloody fact. Thy sisters teach. Bloody woman's job is that. Good God. They spend more time on bloody holiday than they do in front o' their class. God Christ—I could teach as much as they do and still run this entire bloody farm meself. (36)

Moreover, he views his son Arthur's interest in poetry as an unhappy and unhealthy consequence of his wife's indulgence: she "bloody immortalized that lad ... thought he was bloody Shakespeare"(38). Even Slattery himself was apparently taken in by his wife's grossly distorted perception of their son as superior, despite Arthur's persistent academic failures. "When he failed every examination that'd ever been invented," Slattery still believed that Arthur was a "genius" and could not travel the "same road" that was designed for the rest of humanity. Finally one day the farmer, "sweating i' the bloody fields—looked over the bloody hedge" and saw Arthur "lying on his back—composing bloody sonnets. God Christ. Never twigged it. Not till then. Slave me bloody gut out and there he was, twiddling his bloody thumbs and rhyming bloody moon with June" (38–39).

This is indeed a familiar Storey depiction of the hard-working father discovering that his physically capable son is involved in the soft and seemingly barren world of artistic creation. That world, to Slattery, as to Storey's own father, was incomprehensible—it was unmanly, unproductive, and deserving of condemnation.[14]

To Slattery, that moment of peering over the "hedge" had provided him with all the insight needed to dispel any notion that Arthur possessed useful talent. Moreover, the truth of that perception, as least as far as Slattery was concerned, was emphasized in the sweat on his brow in sharp contrast to Arthur's apparent indolence. While he labored, his son twiddled "his bloody thumbs" (38), and, to make matters worse, Arthur's aesthetic efforts were praised by his mother. Such undeserved praise, in Slattery's judgment, led to Arthur's aimless and unproductive adulthood where, according to the farmer, his son "never done a day's bloody work. Not all his life" (36).

Clearly Slattery's deep respect for hard work has not carried over to his children. He has even become suspicious of his wife who now attends "night-school" and, in the opinion of her daughter Wendy, is trying to fight the advance of old age by sharing the "effervescence" of her children. Such behavior separates Slattery from his wife, whom he now views as having lost her direction in life. The farmer is explicit as he complains to his daughters about their "daft" mother. She is "trying to learn at night school all she's known for fifty bloody years—and from men half her bloody age at that—learnt nowt by but what thye've read inside a book"(6).

But what deeply disturbs Slattery—what he most complains bitterly about—is that none of his children has produced children of their own. There is a sense of waste,

of a family disappearing into oblivion.[15] Like Shaw and
Pasmore, Slattery has educated his children, but they have
turned into something quite unnatural in his eyes. On
his farm Slattery fears that the very continuity of his
family has been threatened. To the farmer, the function
of healthy "young women" is "to have babies" and this is
a natural process. "Comes naturally," Slattery addresses
his three daughters, "as bloody breathing. Your own nature's enough to tell you that" (6).

The notion that the family is being disfigured into an
unnatural growth that is incapable of reproducing is further depicted by the dramatist in daughter Jenny's dream
of the family as represented by an "animal with seven
heads":

JENNY. It's [the family] like one, huge corporeal mass. I often dream
of it at night—a sort of animal with seven heads . . .
WENDY. Seven?
JENNY. Don't know why. Only six of us at present. (26)

But we do know why. Since there are only six family
members—the three daughters, one son, and two parents—the seventh head appears excessive until we realize
that it obviously belongs to young Arthur's fiancée,
Alison (38), a forty-two-year-old ex-actress with two children from a previous marriage. Alison's impending marriage to Arthur will in fact add children to the Slattery
family, but they will not come from his bloodline.
Moreover, Arthur is at the time twenty-one, unemployed,
and apparently has no idea where his next job will come
from.

Slattery asks his son how he will support a wife and
her two children. Unfazed by his situation, Arthur simply
replies: "I'll get a job" (39). It is these details that fill out
the image of Jenny's dream of the family as an "animal

with seven heads"—an unnatural entity that has been created, at least as far as Slattery is concerned, by the failure of his children to function normally—that is to say, to pursue productive careers through physical labor and to have families of their own.

Adding to the play's complexity is the suggestion at the end that at least one daughter, Brenda, the youngest and the most rebellious, may in fact redeem the viability of the family through a possible marriage to a most unlikely candidate, the factory worker Albert, with whom she has apparently been having an affair (16). Interestingly, Albert, in his physicality and hardness, resembles Slattery and like the farmer believes that the unmarried status of Brenda and her sisters is unnatural (13).

Nevertheless Albert arrives surreptitiously at Brenda's home in the evening, as he is obviously ashamed at being discovered by her family (11). He even hangs up the phone without acknowledging himself if someone other than Brenda picks up the receiver when he calls (12). Brenda's interest in the young man is at least initially explained by her interest in introducing radical politics to factory workers. She gave a book about "psychology" to Albert's father, "a fifty-five year-old workman," a gift that Arthur thought was "bloody daft" (16); and she even attempted to organize the workers to "strike" in order to take control of the factory where they were employed (33). Nevertheless, Brenda, committed to social activism, becomes involved with Albert, who sees her simply as a woman who should at her age be married with "kiddies" (14). Albert tells Brenda that his "sister got married when she was seventeen" and already has "three kiddies now" (14). However, despite Albert's obvious interest in Brenda and her less explicit interest in him, there is considerable ambiguity at the play's conclusion, as it is not clear that Albert and Brenda will marry and produce the grandchildren that will save the Slattery family bloodline from extinction.

In this regard, Hutchings argues that *The Farm* is static in its structure since "the play ends with a return to the status quo that prevailed at the beginning: Arthur ... has been driven out of the family ... and Albert ... is welcomed at the family table ... as if indeed *h e* were a member of the family itself" (*The Plays* 107). Hutchings then suggests that *The Farm* is an "inversion of Christ's parable of the prodigal son: there is neither forgiveness nor a joyous welcome for the wastrel who returns to the fold, and there will be no feasting in his honor, since the wedding that he planned to announce will not take place" (*The Plays* 107).

In the first place, we cannot tell from the text whether Arthur will or will not marry. When he departs from home, he does so not to break off his engagement to Alison, but to get away from his father, whom he believes is grossly insensitive and incapable of change:

ARTHUR. I brought her [Alison] here—hoping that time might have changed, if not your character [Slattery's], at least your manner. It seems nothing's got better—if anything, it's got far worse. I don't know why I troubled even to think of coming back. (51)

Further, Storey has structurally stationed Albert at both the beginning (11–16) and the end of the drama (59–60); in a sense he sandwiches the play between the appearances of the vital young working man. Unlike Arthur's fiancée, who never shows up, Albert finally does appear, even though he is uninvited. He had previously avoided meeting the family, probably because he felt that his humble circumstances would not be welcomed by the parents of educated daughters. Somehow he has found the courage to present himself at the front door, and his welcome, particularly from Slattery, is both joyous and warm. If the prodigal son Arthur has fled the farm, he has been replaced by a potential son-in-law, Albert, a robust young man who suggests the possibility of family continuity.

The return of Albert undeniably introduces a note of possible redemption—perhaps the family shall be saved. It is of course not at all clear that someone as politically active and as sophisticated as Brenda could ever actually marry someone as limited as Albert, but the suggestion is there and the young factory worker represents, for Slattery at least, a measure of hope that his family shall not disappear.

The play, in fact, ends, despite Hutchings's comments to the contrary (*The Plays* 107), in a most "joyous" scene as Slattery warmly welcomes Albert to the breakfast table and gives him "a bowl o' bloody porridge" while the family begins laughing and eating (60).

In spite of Albert, however, the drama must also be seen as depicting the family as an institution in very deep trouble. Slattery and his wife are no longer a unit, and there is even the suggestion that Mrs. Slattery may be romantically involved with one of her lecturers, "a disenchanted" and "divorced" man of "forty-four" (3). Son Arthur is apparently headed into a disastrous marriage, if he marries at all, and there is no sense in the play that he will ever find direction or even gainful employment in his life. At least two of the daughters have no apparent interest in marrying, and even if Brenda, the youngest, "a fierce girl of twenty-three" (3), does marry the possibility that such a union with Albert would be sustained over any significant period of time is very slim.

Finally Slattery himself has turned to alcohol to survive and has already suffered "a stroke" (19). The Slattery family, despite the possible inclusion of Albert as a son-in-law, is in trouble. The notion that it is dying out or has been twisted into an unnatural creation incapable of reproducing like the—"animal with seven heads" in

Jenny's dream (26)—powerfully overshadows the suggestion that young and robust Albert will come to its rescue.

Storey has also examined the family in two dramas where he has incorporated specific literary influences. In both these plays there is an absence of class division between working-class parents and their university-educated children. Nevertheless, the image of the family that emerges in *Mother's Day* (1976) and in *Early Days* (1980) is, if anything, even bleaker than the image that is created in the three previous dramas where family cohesion is undermined by class division.

In *Mother's Day* (1976) Gordon, the youngest son and most sexually aggressive member of the eccentric Johnson household, makes the following observation about his own family: "This family needs looking into, I can tell you that" (190). This is the richest dramatic understatement in the entire Storey canon.

The mother, Mrs. Johnson, is the central and sole source of family power, controlling her husband, whom she allows in their bedroom only at specified times during the day (191), and her children, including her daughter Lily, a virtual slave, who is forced to spend most of her time in a cupboard.   Her son Harold is home on leave from his Royal Air Force base to prevent his brother Gordon from murdering their father. While at home, Harold decides to leave the military and his own home in order to marry his sister Edna, despite his mother's admonition: "You don't have to leave home to fuck your sister" (243). Finally, Gordon is a rapist who openly boasts about his conquests while his behavior is not only excused but warmly praised by his mother (208).

Into this exceedingly bizarre family, Storey introduces a young and innocent woman, Judy, whose husband has rented a room at the Johnson's. Judy almost immediately becomes the victim of a sexual assault by Gordon (207).

Storey's strategy here is to introduce to the farcical drama a sacrificial victim whose mistreatment would expose the criminality of the family itself. Unfortunately the play limps along, its humor smothered under the details of its complex and clumsy plot.

Mother's Day is an uncharacteristic Storey work whose usual naturalism and close fascination with the details and motivations of working-class families are now transmuted into farce. Storey has obviously been influenced by the farces of Joe Orton, particularly his *Entertaining Mr. Sloan* (1964), as noted in the play's critical reception.[16]

Interestingly, Storey even employs Orton's explicitly inflated language—characters speak with a prodigious sense of propriety while engaging in the most heinous criminal acts (Lahr 106). Consider Gordon's introduction of himself to Judy whom he is about to rape:

GORDON. . . . My mother comes from a titled family. She's the daughter of a famous Lady. Her father was a Lord. They lived in a large house in the country. One day my father—younger than he is now—came to paint the windows. He put the ladder up one morning, saw my mother lying naked on her bed: climbed in, fucked her, and two nights later they eloped. Her father disowned her. They've been together ever since. (186)

Similarly Farrer, Judy's husband, introduces himself to the Johnson family in equally decorous language that masks his criminal purposes. Farrer, who is legally married, is a trickster who pretends to marry young girls like Judy in order to extort money from their wealthy parents (203):

FARRER. I'm employed—in an executive capacity—to look after the interests of certain companies who—for reasons of trade etiquette and business decorum—prefer to have their names unknown, except to certain privileged clients. Perhaps you'll become one of them, Mrs. Johnson, and I can let you into the secrets too! (207)

Moreover, Storey's plot, "the sexual exploitation of a lodger," is the same as Orton's plot in *Entertaining Mr. Sloan* (Hutchings, *The Plays* 110–11). However there are critical differences between the two plays, particularly in the conception of character and in the consistency of the works' farcical tone.

In *Mother's Day* Judy alone possesses none of the farcical elements that define the other characters, and, as such, she is conceptually, even jarringly, out of place within the bizarre world created by Storey. Her sanity is uninteresting and flat—there is really nothing to her, except her presence as a sacrificial victim in the Johnson household. She is there to expose the pathology of those around her—she is there to be sexually exploited.

Orton's Sloan, however, is both a victim and a perpetrator who continues to surprise us as he diplomatically negotiates his way out of difficulties with Kath and her brother Ed, even though, in a burst of passion, he has murdered their father Kem (26–27). The murder itself, unlike the repeated rapes in *Mother's Day*, becomes a pivotal plot device, enabling both Kath and her brother to continue to share Sloan's sexual favors.

For one thing, they now have Sloan in a form of bondage, since they will not hand him over to the police as long as he maintains his sexual availability. Brother Ed, who wishes to keep Sloan at his home, manages to reconcile himself successfully with his sister, who fears the loss of the sexually promiscuous young man. Ed tells his sister: "You've had him six months; I'll have him the next six. I'm not robbing you of him permanently" (148). Even in the aftermath of the brutal murder of their own father, Orton's characters maintain their propriety and negotiate with a sense of decorous protocol that masks their venal interests. Orton's farce, regardless of the absurd conduct of its characters, comments very directly upon the nature of human behavior, particularly in its capacity to deceive while maintaining an outwardly correct posture. John Lahr has observed of Joe Orton:

> All of Orton's characters speak in the same idiom. Their syntax is a model of propriety; their lives are models of impropriety. The very act of speaking demonstrates the thin line between reason and rapacity, which is the mischievous paradox that all Orton's comedies explore. (106)

In Storey's farce, however, the focus upon character disappears, and the play's energy is committed to an increasingly intricate plot, the unraveling of which is considerably more tedious than humorous. In effect, the events themselves in *Mother's Day* take over and become the drama's propelling force, its dramatic raison d'être. Despite its farcical intent, *Mother's Day* becomes humorless—an exhausting exercise in disentangling layer upon layer of complication.

There is also a genuine lack of delicacy in the tone that Storey employs in constructing his farce. Characters move in and out of the farcical structure, often interrupting the flow of the comedy by repetitious and uncharacteristically harsh language—language that would perhaps be appropriate in a naturalistic play. Most notably this occurs in Mrs. Johnson's constant reprimand of her daughter Lily. Every time the two are together the mother immediately shouts "liar" to anything her submissive and terrified daughter utters (177+). This tedious admonition jars painfully on the ear, disrupting the tone of the farce, and is characteristic of a general lack of consistency in the conception of Storey's characters in his play. In Orton's farce, the characters maintain their propriety, regardless of their egregious behavior, and this delicate relationship between the venal and the decorous comments pointedly upon the elusive line that masks private criminality from public correctness.

As a dramatist, Storey is more effective in *Early Days* (1980), a very short play written specifically for the actor Ralph Richardson (Hutchings, *The Plays* 144).[17] Here Storey creates a mysterious elderly gentleman in Sir Richard Kitchen as he reflects upon experiences of his early childhood in an attempt to understand who he is and who the individuals are, including members of his own family, with whom he presently lives. These recollections, which introduce and end the play, also intrude intermittently in the text and principally evoke Sir Richard's memory of abandonment by his parents as a young child (11, 29). More importantly, the profound effect of that early abandonment has not diminished in the course of Sir Richard's life, but has intensified, defining all future human relationships as enigmatic.

At the very beginning of *Early Days*, in the drama's initial monologue, Sir Richard remembers a journey in a "coach" when, as a youngster, he traveled "beneath a bridge":

Beyond the bridge is a beach, which lies in a bay which is surrounded by houses. . . . At some point earlier in the journey I have been left alone on a station platform; or, find that I am alone and those that have been with me are there no longer. (11)

What this memory suggests and what the play demonstrates is the sudden perception that one, like the young child in the recollection, has been abandoned and is fundamentally alone. This disquieting experience persists into adulthood and is expressed as a permanent condition of estrangement.

Sir Richard later recalls that his parents did indeed return, but what results from the reunion is not a sense of security but a vision that sharply reinforces the perception that his interaction with the "multitude" of humanity shall be severely limited and structured by the impossibility of ever truly knowing the other. Adding details, Sir Richard later elaborates upon his early memory:

KITCHEN: The very first time I was lost on a station. There was a very large crowd. When I turned round my parents had gone. I thought at the time they were gone for good. . . . All those strange faces were gazing down. (*Pause.*) A few moments later my parents came back. We mounted a bus. It passed beneath a bridge. . . . Beyond the bridge I saw the sea . . . I was wondering why I was thinking of those early times. It's as if my parents never came back—as if none of our parents ever come back and throughout our lives we stand, looking up at a multitude of faces, not one of which we shall ever know. (29)

If anything, those closest to him, his daughter Mathilda and hated son-in-law Benson, as well as his granddaughter Gloria, whom Sir Richard claims to love, intensify his separation.   Simply put, the members of Kitchen's family cannot know who he is and he cannot know who they are. They too are part of the "multitude of faces" that he saw as a boy and has come to realize are essentially unknowable.   Moreover, the very proximity generated by family relations sharpens rather than blurs the divisions among family: the distressing fact that the members of his family are part of the mysterious "multitude" staring at him can only intensify his estrangement.   Not to know who a stranger is is one thing; not to know who your children are is quite a different matter.

Life, as suggested by the abandoned child, remains a condition of distancing, the return of the parents only adding to the complexity of the dilemma. Indeed, as Sir

Richard comments, "none of our parents ever" truly return (29), and thus the primal sense of separation only introduces him to the persistent condition of estrangement. What returns is a physical presence. They are recognizable as his parents, for "later" his "parents came back," but they are no longer knowable. The parents whom Kitchen had known prior to their abandonment of him have returned as strange as the "multitude" surrounding the boy. This perception takes *Early Days* into the shadowy and mysterious world of Beckett and Pinter. Character is unknowable and the members of one's family, despite blood ties, are like strangers in the street.

In addition, as Sir Richard ages, he also becomes increasingly vulnerable. He is now dependent upon his children for his basic maintenance, and his personal freedom in this humiliating relationship is sharply curtailed. He is required to account for his most basic needs.[18] For example, Benson implicitly threatens Kitchen about his precarious status in the family: "There are worse places you could stay, Father. Without a family atmosphere" (26). The notion of "family atmosphere" as represented by the Benson household is bitterly ironic here, as Kitchen's situation is, by any standard of measurement, a form of imprisonment.

He is forced to endure Bristol, who is employed ostensibly as a companion (14) but is under instructions to report his behavior to his daughter and son-in-law. Kitchen even has no control over his own money and when he asks the gardener to buy him a bottle, the money, on his daughter's instructions, is promptly turned over to her, forcing Sir Richard to think that the money was stolen (21). Most cruelly, Kitchen is sharply reprimanded by his own granddaughter Gloria,[19] who informs him that the very house he lives in belongs to her parents and to her parents alone, and that he is maintained simply on her mother and father's "sufferance" (36).

To a considerable extent, Sir Richard has himself provoked these sharp rebukes because of his eccentric behavior. He has publicly exposed himself in the village and urinated against the wall of a house while its occupant, a "woman ... watched"(24), and has abused Benson at his office by leaving a string of obscenities on his son-in law's telephone answering machine, making certain that the tape would be heard by Benson's employees (25). This behavior is clearly reminiscent of the antisocial behavior of Tommy Pasmore who has taken to petty theft during his retirement in *The March on Russia* (48).

In both cases, however, such behavior is an assertion of self in an intolerable condition: in Pasmore's case, it is an effort to confront the tedium of his retirement, where every day bleeds indistinguishably into the next day, and the only change marking "Sunday" from the rest of the week is the absence of the milkman's delivery (11); in Kitchen's case, it is clearly an effort, however futile, to liberate himself from the imprisonment imposed upon him by his own family.

Like *Mother's Day*, *Early Days* reflects Storey's willingness to experiment with dramatic idiom. The worlds of Samuel Beckett and Harold Pinter are much more accommodating for Storey's talents than the world of Joe Orton, for Sir Richard does possess those enigmatic qualities that infuse a Beckett or Pinter hero with a fundamentally mysterious identity. Nevertheless, *Early Days* is not successful drama.[20] Storey has not found the dramatic metaphor to represent Kitchen's predicament.

For example, Beckett's *Krapp's Last Tape* is a play of memory, similar in conception to *Early Days*. Krapp, "a wearish old man" communicated with himself when he was thirty-nine (18) through the device of a tape recorder.

Kitchen, unfortunately, must rely solely upon his own memory, and we only hear his reflections as he utters them upon the stage. Krapp, on the other hand, is able to communicate directly with himself—to listen directly to himself speaking as a younger man—and Beckett is able to add the additional complexity of an individual not only finding his present experience in life enigmatic, but even finding his former self mysterious. Quite amusingly, Krapp must resort to a dictionary to understand his use of "viduity" (18) when he was a younger man.

No such structural device defining Kitchen's estrangement presents itself in Storey's play. Nor, for that matter, is there any action in *Early Days*, except for Sir Richard's periodic reflections on his perplexity and alienation. In fact, *Early Days* is quite literally a play in which nothing happens. Even Kitchen's brief flight into town where he is found rather quickly and uneventfully by Steven, Gloria's bland fiancé, hardly constitutes a coherent dramatic event (44).[21] Finally, with the exception of Gloria, the other characters are one-dimensional—they lack any complexity in their own right. Bristol is there to serve and to spy on Sir Richard, and Benson and Mathilda to threaten him. It is Kitchen alone who provokes interest, but he himself is not sufficiently complex to sustain the entire play.

Nevertheless, *Early Days* does extend Story's depiction of the family as a treacherous and even cannibalistic environment. As Kitchen ages, his family becomes more predatory than nurturing. In addition, the very fact that the family members are recognizable only intensifies the horror of Kitchen's perception that he is surrounded by a "multitude" of strangers. Our parents, as Kitchen reflects, do return, but they return as strangers, and this strangeness penetrates deeply, undermining the context of all family relationships. This experience of separation represents perhaps Storey's darkest insight into the family: the knowledge that the other family members, despite blood ties, are, like the surrounding multitude, unknowable.

Not all of Storey's family dramas are as bleak as *Early Days*. Indeed in his naturalistic working-class plays there are admirable characters, particularly in the parents who make immense sacrifices for their children. But these sacrifices have born bitter fruit. The children in their professional lives discover to their horror the emptiness of middle-class respectability. Harry Shaw and Tommy Pasmore have not only been exploited as coal miners, but the very purpose of their sacrifices amounts to a further level of exploitation. Quite simply, the very world that their children enter is empty and unfulfilling. The parents have in a sense been grossly deceived, and their children are victimized by a terrible guilt over the enormity of their parents' deception.

In *The Farm*, Slattery expresses essentially the same point of view toward middle-class respectability that is expressed by Shaw's and Pasmore's children. Here, if anything, the Slattery family has grown into something quite unnatural, "an animal with seven heads," and the children's failure to marry and produce children of their own is an expression of the impotence and barrenness of their lives.

In *Mother's Day* the family is depicted as a criminally insane institution, and in *Early Days* it is unknowable and predatory. In Storey's world, the family is clearly not the place to return to when one is in need of nurturing and protection.

NOTES

1. Since the two plays, it will be argued, are companion pieces, they will be discussed together without regard to the chronological separation between their respective productions in 1969 and 1989.

2. If Andrew can display the qualities of an angry young man in *In Celebration*, then Slattery, as Hutchings observed, can equally display the qualities of "An Angry Old Man" in *The Farm* (Plays 101).

3. Curiously Kitchen is the son of a grocer (50), but that fact is completely out of keeping with the tone and detail of the rest of the play. It is mentioned briefly in depicting the details of Sir Richard's early childhood, but the drama itself is solely concerned with an affluent family and the fate of its patriarch, "the longest serving Minister of Health" who was "given a knighthood" (50).

4. The three sons in *In Celebration* are replaced by two daughters and a son in *The March on Russia*. Only Colin Shaw, the one child who does not experience a gender change, resurfaces in the latter play as Colin Pasmore, a university lecturer from his previous incarnation as a smug labor mediator in the automobile industry. Storey, interestingly, has also devoted a novel to Colin and his family, *Pasmore* (1972).

5. Shaw earlier comments on the doorman of The Excelsior, the hotel in which the anniversary dinner is held, as one who used to work for him in the pits. Now the very same man is an object of ludicrous derision: "Do you know the man on the door, dressed up like an admiral—that much braid and epaulets on that he knocks your eye out whenever he turns round—he used to work for me" (37).

6. We learn in *In Celebration* that the father's crawl space in the seam in the mine where he is currently digging out coal—a man of almost sixty-five years of age—is only "thirteen inches" high (64).

7. Storey's own father, a miner, suffered from silicosis (Duffy 68).

8. See Albert Wertheim, who argues that *In Celebration* is representative of the "modern repertoire" of homecoming plays that was inititated with T. S. Eliot's *The Family Reunion* (152). He further argues that these plays, which also include Sam Shepard's *Buried Child* and Harold Pinter's *The Homecoming* all use the "homecoming motif" for a variety of effects (151-152). In particular, Wertheim argues that Andrew in *In Celebration* comes home not to honor his

parents' fortieth wedding anniversary but to celebrate rather "their forty years of guilt-ridden marriage" (159).

9. The fact that the anniversary celebrations for which the families have assembled in both plays occur offstage is similar to offstage events in other Storey plays: the marriage ceremony in *The Contractor* and the rugby match in *The Changing Room*.

10. Andrew's fury is in part also intensified because as a young child he was, at the birth of a new baby, temporarily sent out of his house to be cared for in the home of a neighbor and feels as a result that he was "never" a part of the family (79).

11. Not only have the parents aged twenty years, but so have the children, who are now, with the exception of Colin, who is forty-nine, in their fifties.

12. The fact that Pasmore has begun stealing after having lived a long and honorable life is a dramatic reminder of how empty and unbearable his situation in retirement has become. For the Pasmores every day is alike except Sunday, because on Sunday the "milkman" makes no delivery (11).

13. Interestingly, two critics have had identical reactions to the significance of the two plays: Lindsay Anderson identifies *In Celebration* as Storey's *Long Day's Journey into Night* (*Casebook* 9) while Kimball King identifies *The March on Russia* as Storey's *Long Day's Journey into Night* (*Casebook* 219).

14. Storey recounts a similar confrontation with his own father in "Writers on Themselves" (160) ; moreover, Storey has depicted this situation in his poem "Piano" (*Storey's Lives* 61-62) and most recently in *Stages* (187).

15. The Slattery family resembles the Ewbank family in *The Contractor* where the notion that a family's continuity has been curtailed by its children's unwillingness to produce offspring.

16. Oleg Kerensky, who alone among the critics praises *Mother's Day*, points out, nonetheless, that it was the first Storey play "to get a really bad reception from the critics" (12). Storey himself was so angered by the negative critical reception that he actually assaulted the critic Michael Billington in the lounge of The Royal Court Theatre. See Mel Gussow's "When Writers Turn the Tables Rather Than the Other Cheek" (5-H).

17. Indeed, *Early Days*, although completed in 1974, was not produced until 1980 because of Ralph Richardson's reluctance to perform

the role of Sir Richard. Richardson no longer trusted the "reliability of his own memory" to learn the lines and it was only under the combined urging of Peter Hall and Lindsay Anderson that he agreed to do the role (Hutchings, *The Plays* 144).

18. A similar situation emerges in Pinter's *No Man's Land* (1975). In Pinter's play, however, Hirst, an elderly gentleman similar to Sir Richard Kitchen, is cared for by two somewhat brutal younger men, Foster and Briggs. The two men, moreover, are not family members, but servants, whose exact responsibilities are never made particularly clear; nevertheless, just as Kitchen is dependent upon his daughter and son-in-law for survival, so Hirst is dependent upon the two mysterious young men. Pinter introduces a note of random terror, particularly as it affects Hirst's guest Spooner, while Storey, in a much less successful play, probes the terror of dependence within the context of family relationships.

19. Aside from Kitchen, Gloria is the only character in the play that demonstrates a level of complexity. She clearly loves her grandfather and is, alone among the characters, able to chat affectionately with him (33–34) and is happy to introduce him to her fiancé (36). Moreover, when Benson threatens to place Kitchen "in a strait jacket," after he had fled to the village, Gloria observes that Kitchen has "lived in one all his life" and his fleeing to town represents an effort at freedom (50). Gloria at least has understanding of her grandfather's sense of imprisonment, but like her mother and father she can as well be insensitive and even brutal, as evidenced by her observation that her grandfather is maintained purely upon her parents' "sufferance."

20. The critical reception to the play was "mixed" with most of the reviewers finding merit only in Sir Ralph Richardson's superb performance (John Russell Brown 90-91).

21. One critic argues that *Early Days* is more of a "poem" in which Kitchen's character "unfolds in a measured way" yet remains "mysterious" (Brown 90–91).

5

CONCLUSION:
A TENTATIVE ASSESSMENT

Starting in 1967 with *The Restoration of Arnold Middleton*, Storey has completed fifteen plays, establishing himself as a prolific and inventive playwright. Nevertheless, this present assessment is tentative, since Storey in the sixth decade of his life[1] is still véry much active as a dramatist, having produced two new dramas recently, *The March on Russia* in 1989 and *Stages* in 1992. In addition, if his two latest works indicate anything, they indicate his willingness to experiment in dramatic form. Quite simply, no two plays in the entire Storey canon are as different from each other as these two, and yet each in its own way further expands upon familiar Storey territory—the world of the family in *The March on Russia* and the world of madness in *Stages*.

The March on Russia is a conventional family drama resonating with the literary influence of Ibsen in its slow revelation of character and its exploration of motivation. *Stages*, on the other hand, is a play of recall, similar to Beckett's *Krapp's Last Tape*, in its treatment of memory and its investigation of character as fundamentally enigmatic. Structurally it is a long one-act play, comprised of a series of Richard's monologues as well as his encounters with characters both real and imagined. Moreover, it is not developed within the detailed focus in which character is probed and motivation analyzed that defines the landscape of Storey's naturalistic dramas, among which *The March on Russia* is an example. This observation alone demonstrates the playwright's experimental concerns, since there is no other play in Storey's entire canon that is similar in conception and structure to *Stages*.

Storey clearly will resist the temptation to lock himself into a previous or "safe" mode of dramatic expression. In fact, the playwright's entire career has demonstrated a constant search for new structures and the artistic resourcefulness needed to develop those structures. Storey is only predictable in that he will probably continue to explore the territory of the three worlds outlined in this study (madness, work, and the family), but his new plays, based upon the experimental nature of his previous works, will most likely involve new and inventive techniques. Indeed, such future contributions may yet enhance David Storey's reputation as an experimental dramatist.

Of course, the development of a playwright, or any artist for that matter, is not incremental in qualitative terms. Playwrights, however talented, do not necessarily write better plays at the conclusion of their careers. Chronology is less important than the willingness to experiment and to take chances. Some of Storey's finest plays like *The Contractor*, *Home*, and *The Changing*

Room, occurred relatively early in his career, in 1969, 1970, and 1972 respectively. At any rate, even if Storey never writes another play—which is, as has been argued, most unlikely—his reputation as a dramatist is secure.

In this study Storey's plays have been grouped into three separate categories that represent the focus of his dramatic concerns and development: the worlds of madness, work, and the family. Within each of these categories Storey's work has been examined chronologically following the date of the play's production. This approach has allowed us to isolate similar types of plays and to study their development chronologically, and there have been obvious advantages in proceeding in this manner. For example, we could watch Storey's developing understanding of the complexity of madness to the point where madness itself is sharpened into a tool for survival. We can focus on Storey's fascination with detail in the work process, whether that process involved the construction of a tent, the warm-up of a rugby team, or instruction in drawing from the nude model. Or we could examine the tensions emerging in family relationships, particularly when social class divides children from their parents. Obviously the three strands of development were useful in examining the playwright's growth, but Storey must ultimately be judged as a dramatist with a unified body of work. To that end, we must merge the three strands of work together and assess Storey's plays as a single contribution.

Storey is most successful as a dramatist when he discovers within his play the precise image that defines and controls the emerging theme of his drama. This image may in fact be a physical structure and process like the beautiful wedding marquee and its erection and disassembly in *The Contractor*. Here the tent is painstakingly set up, flutters briefly in its completed glory, and is then unceremoniously disassembled. All that is left are three bare tent poles upon the stage (246).

The tent and its disassembly comments directly upon the probable impermanence of Maurice and Claire's marriage and the fragility inherent in all relationships, including the camaraderie of the workers themselves, as specifically demonstrated in the sudden cooling of Fitzgerald's and Marshall's close friendship. On a deeper level, the tent reflects the probable severing of the Ewbank family line, from the grandfather, a proud maker of rope, to Ewbank the contractor, gruff and efficient, to his offspring, Claire, who is phlegmatically entering into an apparently disastrous marriage, and Paul, who is curiously unconcerned about his lack of direction or purpose. The once proud and robust Ewbank family itself will disappear, its impending demise represented in the spiritless lives of its sole heirs, Claire and Paul Ewbank.

The image may also be individuals like the rugby players who merge before us into a team in *The Changing Room*. As the tent served as the unifying and controlling image in *The Contractor*, so the rugby players themselves in *The Changing Room* function in the same symbolic manner. As the team evolves, the individual characteristics of the team members, all sharply delineated as they appear initially on stage, dissolve and in the process the men merge into a rugby team. Out of the flesh of the individual athletes, the team is created, each member now subsumed in its collective entity. What was an array of individual men with specific personalities is now a uniformed and unified force, an athletic team, each individual member indistinguishable from the others. Moreover, at the conclusion of the match, the men undress, removing their uniforms, and bathe, washing away the dirt and grime collected in their fierce athletic encounter. This bathing completes the ritual, as the team itself now dissolves, the men returning to their individual selves. The men now dress, their idiosyncratic characteristics emerging in both the manner of their dressing and the style of their clothes. The competitive team has disappeared. Now separate and distinct, the men return home.

As a team, the men ready themselves in pregame warm-ups to engage in competition, and a sense of danger is projected from the group's focus and drive. On the field these men can and will be very committed competitors, sacrificing themselves on behalf of the team's effort. In so doing they will engage in the rough and dangerous game of professional rugby. There will be violence committed on the field, as evidenced in Kendal's injury and the numerous cuts and bruises of the other players. This violence arises out of the compelling energy and necessity of team sport and would not occur if the men were acting alone. What Storey has indeed shown us is the ritual of the birth of a team, a unified and dangerous force, and its subsequent dispersal into the separate lives of its players.

Another use of individuals as controlling images occurs in the very dark final moments of *Home* when two men, Harry and Jack, both schizophrenic patients, stare out at us, the audience, and see in the so-called sane world the potential menace to destroy civilization itself (82). Now existence itself is in harm's way and the creator will not, in the view of these two men, pause to intervene. Jack, who once thought of becoming a priest (16), assures us that creation itself was a mistake, and the creator will not make that particular "mistake" again (82). As the two men stare out at us, Alfred, who has been lobotomized, continues to remove the remaining props, "the two wicker chairs" (82), and the two men are left upon a bleak and empty stage. This is the darkest of all possible apocalyptic statements, and Storey has found in the final closing moments of his play the perfect stage imagery to encapsulate his theme: the line between sanity and madness is elusive and, more importantly, the potential danger of the sane far exceeds any possible danger associated with the insane.

Tragically, the solution to the problems caused by creation, the primal mistake, will only be fulfilled in the coming disaster. Jack and Harry, both schizophrenic, will be destroyed along with the world that surrounds them. Those who are judged sane possess the tools of devastation.

In addition, as we have seen, Storey has in his most important plays used space effectively, both on- and offstage. He has skillfully projected the tension and imagery flowing between the theatrical space within, what we can perceive, with the theatrical space without, what we can conceive. The importance of the marriage between Maurice and Claire, a most tenuously projected union, which we never actually see, flows in upon the onstage events, shaping and focusing the activities of the entire Ewbank family as well as the personal relationships of the tent erectors in the family's employ. Moreover, the theme of impermanence, enhanced by the offstage marriage, is further reflected in the probable disappearance of the Ewbank family itself through its children's failure to produce children of their own.

In *The Changing Room* the individual members of the rugby team join into a collective, uniformed force on the stage, the theatrical space within, while offstage, the theatrical space without, the noises from the fans are interspersed with fanfare music. The sound and energy offstage clearly function to focus the energy of the onstage team. We now can see both worlds, one directly perceived and one imaginatively conceived, and both worlds contribute to the complex and rich imagery of the team's unification, its subsequent engagement in sport, and finally its dispersal into individuals who leave for home and their private destinies.

Home in many ways is Storey's most brilliant use of space. For initially we are not even aware that the world we view is the world of the insane, so similar is their behavior to ours. Further, the audience, at whom Jack and Harry stare in perplexity and fear, is the sane world that represents an encroaching and menacing force, capable of unimaginable destruction. The world that performs lobotomies upon individuals whose behavior, like Alfred's, is unacceptable, is the sane world that has produced a nuclear arsenal with the potential to erase civilization. The world within, the mental institution and its residents, is threatened by the world without, the very world that erected the mental institution itself. Within the balance of what is occurring onstage and offstage, of what is directly perceived and of what is imaginatively conceived, Storey projects the impending disaster awaiting our civilization.

In these three dramas, there are no central events and no central characters. Indeed, in both *The Contractor* and *The Changing Room* the principal events themselves—the marriage and the rugby match—occur offstage. In *Home* there simply is no central event. It is clearly the principal images created in these plays and their controlling relationship with the activity evolving onstage and offstage that produce a consistently high level of fascination. Moreover, these complex images linger long after the details of each play are forgotten, and they continue to suggest a range of interpretations.

Storey has also written a number of plays that reflect another level of his talent. Plays like *In Celebration, The Farm,* and *The March on Russia* demonstrate Storey's versatility in handling conventional plots within a naturalistic setting. In these plays, by Storey's own admission ("Conversations with David Storey" 49), he has learned from Ibsen the technique of peeling away layers from a character's protective psychological armor to expose the individual's motivation and hypocrisy.

Unlike Ibsen, however, Storey never quite fulfills the potential within these dramas. Andrew's expected confrontation with his mother never occurs, and this represents a serious weakness in *In Celebration*. It is a defect in the play, and Storey's attempt to minimize it by claiming that his plays, unlike Ibsen's, investigate the "bomb ... festering away" rather than Ibsen's investigation of the bomb after it has exploded is somewhat disingenuous ("Conversations with David Storey" 49).

In Celebration demands, as Storey's own brother Anthony observed indirectly in his novel *Brothers Keepers* (64-65), that the confrontation—what Storey means by the bomb "explosion"—occur between Andrew and his mother. The entire play moves toward this central moment of crisis, and the fact that it never occurs seriously minimizes the impact of the drama. The play teases us into an expectation that never occurs. Andrew's energy disperses, and the play ends without any resolution between son and mother.

The fact that a similar confrontation resurfaces and is concluded some twenty years later in 1989 in *The March on Russia* may be interesting and helpful in forming a total understanding of the playwright and in reading his work intertextually, but it certainly does not save *In Celebration* from its irresolution and incompleteness.

These plays are perhaps most interesting because they document the sharp separation that occurs between working-class parents and their university-educated children. Not only do they provide penetrating portraits of the children, like Andrew in *In Celebration*   and

Wendy in *The March on Russia,* but they also expose the paradoxical situation of the parents themselves, particularly the fathers.

For the children believe that they have been doubly victimized by their parents' sacrifices. They have discovered that their world of middle-class respectability is empty, and they have been crippled by the powerful guilt stemming from their parents' prolonged suffering to provide them with their university educations. The fathers, in turn, want their children to succeed, but at the same time detest the very respectable world that their children have entered.

Interestingly, *The Farm,* alone among Storey's conventional plays, has the potential to be listed among the dramatist's most powerful works. For one thing, Slattery, the farmer, is far more compelling as a character than either Shaw or Pasmore. He alone among the fathers is not taken in by the professional status of his children or, as in the case of his son Arthur, their artistic pretensions. Like Ewbank in *The Contractor,* Slattery believes deeply in the enduring merit of his own physical labor and that such labor is the only labor worthy of respect.

There is also within *The Farm* the possible connection between emerging theme and imagery that powerfully occurs in Storey's best plays. The imagery refers to Jenny's dream of the "monster" with seven heads, a direct reference to the Slattery family and its development into a grotesque "huge corporeal mass" (26). For Slattery's children, like Ewbank's children, are apparently destined to be nonproductive—they themselves will not marry and reproduce. Such behavior contributes to the demise of their own family.

Unfortunately, Storey never found the symbol in *The Farm* to represent Jenny's dream. The dream indeed is discussed, and its obvious association with the unhappy destiny of the family is clear, but unlike the erection and disassembly of the tent or the emergence and disappearance of the team, it is never formulated as a controlling and defining dramatic symbol.

Finally Storey has shown a life-long fascination with madness and its representation on the stage as in *The Restoration of Arnold Middleton* and most recently *Stages*.   His close identification with R. D. Laing's interpretation of schizophrenia as a political label rather than a medical one is less important than his dramatization of the elusive line separating madness from sanity and his evolving understanding of the condition of schizophrenia, for individuals like Fenchurch, as a necessary mode of survival.

Nonetheless, Storey's conventional plays do not possess the imagery or inventive power found in his experimental work like *The Contractor* and *The Changing Room*.   They are interesting as dramatic documents of working-class families struggling to survive.   They also represent Chekhov's and Ibsen's influence upon Storey in his handling of naturalistic dramatic material.   As works of dramatic art, however, they do not possess the dramatic intensity of his three major works.

Only two of David Storey's fifteen plays have been excluded from our discussion: *Cromwell* (1973) and *Phoenix* (1984). *Cromwell* is perhaps only interesting in the playwright's use of free verse and his incorporation of a Brechtian structure in his sole historical drama.   The play also suggests, at least in its title, a treatment of puritanism, a subject, as we have seen, of considerable influence upon Storey's dramas and fiction.   Yet Cromwell himself never appears in Storey's play and, as Gindin points out, the play itself in its treatment of the historical material is unclear. Gindin writes: "In specific terms, the play [*Cromwell*] is puzzling, for Proctor, its hero, who always sounds as if he is a Roundhead, loses his farm and child to what are apparently Roundhead marauders and yet is looking for Cromwellian 'light'" (507). Indeed the play drifts off into an excessively abstract journey at its conclusion in Proctor's search for presumably a mode of spiritual liberation from ideological and religious strife, and must be seen, despite its poetic language and fluid use of theater space, as a curious anomaly in Storey's body of work. See Phyllis Randall who comments briefly on the "unique" position of *Cromwell* in the Storey canon, a play incidentally that the playwright himself now sees as a "disaster" (254-55).

Interestingly, *Phoenix*, at least superficially, has the elements of a typical Storey family drama: the hero, Alan Ashcroft, is, like many of Storey's heroes, as well as David Storey himself, an ex-professional athlete (10) and the son of a coal miner (10). Ashcroft has transformed himself into a theater director in the north of England with a willingness to promote the avant-garde despite the hostility of the local community. Thus Ashcroft, like the young David Storey, has made the transition from the world of intense physical confrontation—he is an ex-light heavy-weight boxer (9)—to the aesthetic and intellectually demanding world of the theater. Further, Ashcroft's wife, Christine, from whom he is separated, has been confined to a mental institution (13), a typical Storey family situation in both his fiction and dramas, although during the course of this particular play she is on leave and appears as sane as any of the other characters who people the play.

Nevertheless, despite its rich array of cleverly drawn characters, *Phoenix* is a dramatic diatribe against individuals and institutions who control the funds of subsidized theater in England. Specifically, the real dramatic interest in *Phoenix* is not focused upon the madness of Christine or the family problems of Ashcroft but upon Swallow, who, although well-meaning—he believes he is protecting the financial interests of the hard-working people like coal miners whose taxes support subsidized theater (11)—is intellectually and aesthetically vacuous. Thus, the fate of subsidized British theater lies in the hands of philistines who will frustrate any attempt at sophisticated productions—productions perhaps that please "the sophisticates in London" (11). Finally, the literal explosion at the end of the drama—the theater itself is dynamited (63)—suggests that the only hope for theater is its destruction and, like the fabled phoenix, possible resurrection from its own ashes.

Interestingly, Storey handled the same situation in his novel *Present Times*, published in 1984, the same year as the initial amateur production of *Phoenix*. Clearly the play's intent, like the novel's, is to isolate an individual in a world spinning out of control—the world of London in *Present Times*, the world of the north of England in *Phoenix*. Frank Attercliffe, an ex-professional footballer, saves himself by becoming a playwright while Ashcroft engages in the more symbolic but ultimately pointless act of blowing up his own theater. In the novel, Storey's hero acts decisively to save himself—through the art of playwriting Attercliffe can survive in the maddening chaos of present day London. In the drama, Ashcroft's explosion is ultimately an impotent reaction—an act of rage that saves neither himself nor his theater. Perhaps, of course, that is Storey's principal interest in *Phoenix*: the state of contemporary subsidized theater is so dismal that such theater—quite literally—should be destroyed. But this is precisely what is wrong with the play. It is not clear where Storey's true interest lies: in the crumbling world of

Alan Ashcroft or in the state of subsidized theater. The latter focus is clearly the less interesting as drama and would have perhaps been better expressed directly as an essay.

Nevertheless, *The Contractor*, *The Changing Room*, and *Home* are clearly "the gift of song," Allott's definition in *Life Class* of a work of art (176-77), and their imagery and invention continue to tease our imagination and to stimulate our intellect. At the very least, these dramas defy definitive interpretations. There are always other possible explanations for the tent or the rugby team or Harry and Jack's final appearance on a bleak stage. The multiplicity of interpretation contributes toward the richness of Storey's dramatic technique—dramas that fuse action that we can see onstage with offstage events that we conceptualize into powerful and enduring images, or as Peter Brook has suggested, "lingering silhouettes" (136).

Storey has also shown particular insight in exploring the world of the insane, and demonstrating how the so-called sane world with its lobotomies, its hypocrisy and cruelty, and its nuclear potential is infinitely more dangerous than the world of the insane; moreover, he has isolated mental illness itself upon the stage as a mechanism of survival—the only remaining mechanism for some like Richard Fenchurch—when surrounding conditions become psychologically unendurable.

In his family plays, like *In Celebration* and *The Farm*, Storey has, more incisively and dramatically than any other contemporary dramatist, documented the painful division that exists between working-class parents and their educated and permanently alienated children. Moreover, his understanding of the working class is ex-emplified in the moving portraits he has drawn of men like Shaw, Slattery, and Pasmore. There is no condescension in Storey's portraits—no attempt at easy humor at the expense of these men, however limited they may appear because of the meanness of their circumstances. There is understanding and respect for their difficult lives and their sacrifices for their families. David Storey is truly among the finest working-class playwrights that England has produced in the twentieth century.

Even if David Storey writes nothing else—and this is quite unlikely, since he is a prolific novelist and playwright—his reputation as a major and inventive twentieth-century British dramatist is secure. He clearly deserves our respect and admiration, as well as our continued scholarly and critical interest.

NOTES

1. David Malcolm Storey was born in Wakefield, Yorkshire, 13 July 1933 (Morgan, 556).

SELECTED BIBLIOGRAPHY

PRIMARY WORKS BY DAVID STOREY

Novels

Storey, David. *This Sporting Life*. London: Longman, 1960.

_____. *Flight Into Camden*. London: Cape, 1960.

_____. *Radcliffe*. New York: Coward-McCann, 1964.

_____. *Pasmore*. London: Longman, 1972.

_____. *A Temporary Life*. London: Allen Lane, 1973.

_____. *Saville*. New York: Harper & Row, 1976.

_____. *A Prodigal Child*. New York: Dutton, 1982.

_____. *Present Times*. London: Cape, 1984.

Plays

Storey, David. *The Restoration of Arnold Middleton*. London: Samuel French, 1967.

_____. *In Celebration*. Introd. Ronald Hayman. London: Hereford Play Series, 1973.

_____. *The Contractor. The Changing Room, Home, The Contractor: Three Plays by David Storey.* New York: Avon, 1975.

_____. *Home. The Changing Room, Home, The Contractor: Three Plays by David Storey.* New York: Avon, 1975.

_____. *The Changing Room. David Storey: Home, The Changing Room, Mother's Day.* New York: Penguin, 1984.

_____. *Cromwell.* London: Jonathan Cape, 1973.

_____. *Early Days. Storey: Early Days, Sisters, Life Class.* London: Penguin, 1980.

_____. *The Farm.* New York: Samuel French, 1974.

_____. *Life Class. Storey: Early Days, Sisters, Life Class.* London: Penguin, 1980.

_____. *Mother's Day. David Storey: Home, The Changing Room, Mother's Day.* New York: Penguin, 1984.

_____. *Sisters. Storey: Early Days, Sisters, Life Class.* London: Penguin, 1980.

_____. *The March on Russia.* London: Samuel French, 1989.

_____. *Stages. Storey Plays One: The Contractor, Home, Stages, Caring.* London: Methuen, 1992.

_____. "Caring." *Storey Plays One: The Contractor, Home, Stages, Caring.* London: Methuen, 1992.

_____. *Phoenix.* Woodstock: Dramatic Publishing, 1993.

Essays

Storey, David. "Writers on Themselves: Journey through a Tunnel." *Listener.* August 1963: 159–63.

_____. "Working With Lindsay." *25 Years of the English Stage Company.* Ed. Richard Findlater. New York: Grove Press, 1981. 110–18.

_____. Introduction. *Storey Plays One: The Contractor, Home, Stages, Caring.* London: Methuen, 1992. ix–xii.

Films

Storey, David. *This Sporting Life.* Dir. Lindsay Anderson. With Richard Harris, Rachel Roberts, and Colin Blakely. Continental Films, 1963.

_____. *In Celebration.* Dir. Lindsay Anderson. With Alan Bates. American Film Theater, 1975.

Poetry

Storey, David. *Storey's Lives: Poems 1951-1991.* London: Jonathan Cape, 1992.

_____. "Bella," a poem, published separately in program to *Stages,* provided for Royal National Theatre production, 1992.

PRIMARY WORKS BY WRITERS OTHER THAN DAVID STOREY

Beckett, Samuel. *Endgame.* New York: Grove, 1958.

_____. *Krapp's Last Tape.* New York: Grove, 1958.

_____. *Waiting for Godot.* New York: Grove, 1954.

Chekhov, Anton. *The Cherry Orchard. Anton Chekhov's Plays.* Trans. and ed. Eugene K. Bristow. New York: Norton, 1977.

Eliot, T. S. "The Love Song of J. Alfred Prufrock." *The Complete Poems and Plays: 1909-1950.* New York: Harcourt, 1958.

Horovitz, Israel. *Stage Directions and Spared: The Quannapowitt Quartet, Parts Three and Four.* New York: Dramatists Play Service, 1977.

Lewis, Wyndham. *Rude Assignment: An Intellectual Autobiography.* 1950. Ed. Toby Foshay. Santa Barbara: Black Sparrow, 1984.

Mamet, David. *American Buffalo.* New York: Grove, 1977.

Orton, Joe. *Entertaining Mr. Sloan. The Complete Plays.* New York: Grove, 1976.

Osborne, John. *Look Back in Anger.* New York: Penguin. 1982.

Pinter, Harold. "The Dumb Waiter." *Complete Works: One.* New York: Grove Press, 1976. 127–67.

_____. "The Black and White." *Complete Works: Two.* New York: Grove Press, 1977. 240–43.

_____. *No Man's Land.* New York: Grove Press, 1975.

Shakespeare, William. *Richard II,* Ed. Louis B. Wright and Virginia A. LaMar. New York: Washington Square Press, 1962.

Shepard, Sam. *Buried Child. Seven Plays.* New York: Bantam, 1981.

Storey, Anthony. *Brothers Keepers.* London: Boyars, 1975.

Williams, Tennessee. *A Streetcar Named Desire.* New York: New Directions, 1980.

SECONDARY WORKS

Ansorge, Peter. "The Theatre of Life: David Storey in Interview." *Plays and Players* September 1973: 32–36.

Bedell, Jeanne Fenrick. "Towards Jerusalem: The Changing Portrayal of the Working Class in Modern English Drama, 1900-1970." Diss. Southern Illinois U, 1975.

Billington, Michael. "First Nights: *The Restoration of Arnold Middleton*," *Plays and Players* June 1970: 30.

_____."A Play Worth Having." Rev. of *In Celebration*. *The Times* 23 April 1969: 16A.

Brook, Peter. *The Empty Space*. New York: Atheneum, 1980.

Brown, John Russell. *A Short Guide to Modern British Drama*. London: Heinemann, 1982.

Browne, Terry W. *Playwrights' Theatre: The English Stage Company at The Royal Court Theatre*. London: Pitman, 1975.

Bygrave, Mike. "David Storey: Novelist or Playwright?" *Theatre Quarterly* 1.2 (1971): 31–36.

Carlson, Marvin. *Theatre Semiotics: Signs of Life*. Bloomington: Indiana UP, 1990.

_____. *Theories of the Theatre: A Historical and Critical Survey, from the Greeks to the Present*. Ithaca: Cornell UP, 1984.

Carpenter, Charles A. "Bond, Shaffer, Stoppard, Storey: An International Checklist of Commentary." *Modern Drama* 24 (1981): 546–56.

_____. *Modern British Drama*. Arlington Heights, Il: AHM Publishing, 1979. 88–91.

Cave, Richard A. *New British Drama in Performance on the London Stage: 1970 to 1985*. New York: St. Martin's, 1988.

Clark, Susan Mauk. "David Storey: The Emerging Artist." Diss. Purdue U, 1976.

Cohn, Ruby. *Retreats from Realism in Recent English Drama*. New York: Cambridge UP, 1991.

Dennis, Norman, Fernando Heriques, and Clifford Slaughter. *Coal Is Our Life: An Analysis of a Yorkshire Mining Community*. London: Tavistock, 1969.

Doty, Gresdna A., and Billy J. Harbin. *Inside The Royal Court Theatre, 1956–1981: Artists Talk*. Baton Rouge: Louisiana State UP, 1990.

Duffy, Martha. "An Ethic of Work and Play." *Sports Illustrated* 5 March 1973: 66–69.

Dutton, Richard. *Modern Tragicomedy and the British Tradition*. Norman: U of Oklahoma Press, 1986.

Elam, Keir. *The Semiotics of Theatre and Drama*. 1980. London and New York: Routledge, 1991.

Esslin, Martin. *The Field of Drama: How the Signs of Drama Create Meaning on Stage and Screen*. London: Methuen, 1987.

Feder, Lillian. *Madness in Literature*. New Jersey: Princeton UP, 1980.

Findlater, Richard. ed. *25 Years of the English Stage Company*. New York: Grove Press, 1981.

Flatley, Guy. "I Never Saw a Pinter Play." *New York Times* 29 November 1970, sec. 2: pp. 1, 5.

Free, William J. "The Ironic Anger of David Storey." *Modern Drama* 16 (1973): 307–16.

Gaskill, William A. *A Sense of Direction: Life at The Royal Court Theatre.* 1988. New York: Limelight Edition, 1990.

Gibb, Frances. "Why David Storey Has Got It in for Academics, the Critics, and 'Literary Whizz-Kids." *Times Higher Education Supplement* 4 February 1977: 9.

Gindin, James. "David Storey." *British Dramatists Since World War 11: M-Z.* Vol. 13 of Dictionary of Literary Biography. Ed. Stanley Weintraub. Detroit: Gale Research, 1982. 501–13.

Gray, Paul. "Class Theatre, Class Film: An Interview with Lindsay Anderson." *Tulane Drama Review* 11.1 (1966): 122–125.

Gussow, Mel. "To David Storey, A Play is a Holiday." *New York Times* 20 April 1973: 14.

_____. "When Writers Turn the Tables Rather Than the Other Cheek." *New York Times* 16 July 1989: 5-H.

Guthke, Karl. *Modern Tragicomedy: An Investigation into the Nature of the Genre.* New York: Random House, 1966.

Harris, Judith Dotson. "An Unholy Encounter: The Early Works of David Storey." Diss. Ohio State U, 1974.

Hartnoll, Phyllis, ed. *The Oxford Companion to the Theatre.* 4th ed. London: Oxford UP, 1983.

Hayman, Ronald. *British Theatre since 1955: A Reassessment.* Oxford UP, 1979.

_____. "Conversation With David Storey." *Drama: The Quarterly Theatre Review* 99 (Winter 1970): 47–53.

Heiney, Donald, and Lenthiel Downs. "David Storey." *Contemporary British Literature.* Vol. 2. New York: Barron's, 1974. 208–14.

Hilton, Julian. "The Court and Its Favours: The Careers of Christopher Hampton, David Storey, and John

Arden." *Stratford-upon-Avon Studies, 19: Contemporary English Drama* (1981): 139–55. Rpt. in *Modern British Dramatists: New Perspectives.* Ed. John Russell Brown. Englewood Cliffs: Prentice-Hall, 1984. 50–74.

Hirst, David L. *Tragicomedy.* London: Methuen, 1984.

Hutchings, William. ed. *David Storey: A Casebook.* New York: Garland, 1992.

_____. *The Plays of David Storey: A Thematic Study.* Carbondale: Southern Illinois UP, 1988.

_____. "The Significance of Ritual in the Plays of David Storey." Diss. U of Kentucky, 1981.

Kalson, Albert E. "Insanity and the Rational Man in the Plays of David Storey." *Modern Drama* 19 (1976): 111–29.

Kerensky, Oleg. *The New British Drama: Fourteen Playwrights since Osborne and Pinter.* New York: Taplinger Publishing Company, 1977.

King, Kimball. *Twenty Modern British Playwrights: A Bibliography, 1956 to 1976.* New York: Garland, 1977. 231–39.

Lahr, John. "The Theatre: Laughing It Off." *The New Yorker* 21 February 1994: 106–108.

Laing, R. D. *Knots.* New York: Random House, 1970.

_____. *The Divided Self: An Existential Study in Sanity and Madness.* 1959. Baltimore: Penguin, 1970.

_____. *The Politics of Experience.* New York: Ballantine Books, 1968.

Lambert, J. W. "Plays in Performance." *Drama: The Quarterly Theatre Review* 104 (Spring 72): 14–16.

Morgan, Margery. "David Storey." *Great Writers of the English Language: Dramatists.* Ed. James Vinson. New York: St. Martin's Press, 1979. 556–58.

Morley, Sheridan. *Review Copies: Plays and Players in London, 1970–74.* Totowa: Roman and Littlefield, 1975.

Nightingale, Benedict. "David Storey." *Contemporary Dramatists.* Ed. James Vinson. New York: St. Martin's Press, 1982. 762–65.

_____. *A Reader's Guide to Fifty Modern British Plays.* London: Heinemann, 1982.

Nolan, Ernest Isaiah, III. "Beyond Realism: A Study of Time and Place in the Plays of David Storey." Diss. U of Notre Dame, 1975.

Orr, John. *Tragicomedy and Contemporary Culture: Play and Performance from Beckett to Shepard.* Ann Arbor: U of Michigan Press, 1991.

Pearce, Howard D. "A Phenomenological Approach to the *Theatrum Mundi* Metaphor." 95 *PMLA* (1980): 42–57.

Quigley, Austin E. "The Emblematic Structure and Setting of David Storey's Plays." *Modern Drama* 22 (1979): 259–76.

Randall, Phyllis R. "Division and Unity in David Storey." *Essays on Contemporary British Drama.* Ed. Hedwig Bock and Albert Wertheim. Munich: Hueber, 1981. 253–65.

Reinelt, Janelle G. "The Novels and Plays of David Storey: New Solutions in Form and Technique." Diss. Stanford, 1978.

Rich, Frank. "Critic's Notebook: 3 New British Plays With Serious Messages." *New York Times* 23 December 92: C9+.

Roberts, Philip. *The Royal Court Theatre: 1965–1972.* London: Routledge, 1986.

Rosen, Carol. *Plays of Impasse: Contemporary Drama Set in Confining Institutions.* Princeton: Princeton UP, 1983.

_____.   "Symbolic Naturalism in David Storey's *Home*." *Modern Drama* 22 (1979): 277–89.

Rusinko, Susan. *British Drama: 1950 to the Present*. Boston: Twayne, 1989.

Scolnicov, Hanna. "Theatre Space, Theatrical Space, and the Theatrical Space Without." *Themes in Drama 9: The Theatrical Space*. New York: Cambridge UP, 1987. 11–26.

Shrapnel, Susan. "No Goodness and No Kings." *Cambridge Quarterly* 5 (1970): 181–87.

Stinson, John J. "Dualism and Paradox in the 'Puritan' Plays of David Storey." *Modern Drama* 20 (1977): 131–43.

Styan, J. L. *The Dark Comedy: The Development of Modern Comic Tragedy*. London: Cambridge UP, 1962.

Taylor, John Russell. *David Storey: Writers and Their Work, No. 239*. Edinburgh: Longman, 1974.

_____. *The Second Wave: British Drama of the Sixties*. London: Methuen, 1971.

Torrey, E. Fuller, et al. *Schizophrenia and Manic-Depressive Disorder: The Biological Roots of Mental Illness as Revealed by the Landmark Study of Identical Twins*. New York: Basic Books, 1994.

Wardle, Irving. Rev. of *Home*. *Times*, 18 Jun. 1970. Rpt. in *Plays in Review, 1956–1980: British Drama and the Critics*.   Ed. Careth Evans and Barbara Lloyd Evans. New York: Methuen, 1985. 171.

Weaver, Laura H. "Journey Through a Tunnel: The Divided Self in the Novels and Plays of David Storey." Diss. University of Kansas, 1977.

_____. "Madness and the Family in David Storey's Plays." *David Storey: A Casebook*. Ed. William Hutchings. New York: Garland, 1992.

Wertheim, Albert. "The Modern British Homecoming Play." *Comparative Drama* 19 (1985): 151-65.

The Wooster Group, Inc. *Dionysus in 69.* Ed. Richard Schechner. New York: Farrar, Strauss and Giroux, 1970.

Worth, Katharine J. *Revolutions in Modern English Drama.* London: G. Bell & Son, 1973.

Young, B. A. *The Mirror Up To Nature: A Review of the Theatre: 1964-1982.* London: William Kimber, 1982.

INDEX

About the Author

HERBERT LIEBMAN is Associate Professor of English at The College of Staten Island, City University of New York. He is an NEA Award winning playwright and has published short stories in *Confrontation, Chelsea, Paris Transcontinental, Midstream,* and the Pen Syndicated Fiction Project.

ISBN 0-313-29865-3

EAN

9 780313 298653

HARDCOVER BAR CODE